The Burning of Monterey

The Burning of Monterey

*The 1818 Attack on California by the
Privateer Bouchard*

Peter Uhrowczik

CYRIL
Books

CYRIL Books, Los Gatos, California, 95030
Cyrilbooks@aol.com

Copyright © 2001 Peter Uhrowczik
All rights reserved. Published 2001
Printed in the United States of America

ISBN: 0-970-93520-X
LCCN: 2001135003

Publisher's Cataloging-in-Publication
(Provided by Quality Books, Inc.)
Uhrowczik, Peter.
The burning of Monterey: the 1818 attack on California by
the privateer Bouchard / Peter Uhrowczik.
— 1st ed.
p. cm.
Includes bibliographical references and index.
LCCN: 2001135003
ISBN: 0-970-93520-X
1. Monterey (Calif.)-History. 2. Bouchard, Hipolito. I. Title.
F869.M7U37 2001   979.4'76
QBI01-200670

Contents

Illustrations

Preface

Browsing in a bookstore in Monterey, I overheard an Argentine tourist asking about material on Bouchard's raid on California. "You mean the pirate raid?" said the clerk. "No, not a pirate—he was a patriot," said the visitor. "Well, he was a pirate to us," retorted the Californian.

This piqued my interest. I had a cursory knowledge of the raid but knew very little about Bouchard himself. Who was this man, and why had he come all the way to Monterey? And was he a patriot or a pirate?

The events narrated in this book happened during the Spanish colonial period of Alta California (the period before the Mexican and U.S. rules). It was a time when the famous California missions were at the height of their glory and when the Spanish-American rebels, outside of California, were turning against Spanish domination. Alta California was untouched by the rebellion against Spain until 1818, when Hipólito Bouchard attacked the California coast. Bouchard took Monterey, the capital of Alta California, creating panic throughout the entire province. Who was this man? And why did he come?

The Californians thought Bouchard was a pirate, and they still think of him as such today. But Bouchard was a privateer (a notch above pirate) at the service of the South American insurgents. A privateer commanded a privately armed vessel, authorized by a government to attack an enemy of that government. The newly independent American republics, lacking formal navies, used privateers at length in their struggle for emancipation from colonial rule. The United States used privateers extensively in its wars with Great Britain, and the Spanish-American rebels followed the U.S. example with gusto. Although the wars of American independence are usually described in terms of land engagements, privateering contributed significantly to those wars.

While more has been written about the U.S. and Mexican periods of California history than about the Spanish period, this era provides us with wonderful accounts of sacrifice, bravery, and loyalty to king and Church. The Bouchard raids were important events in this colorful period. They mark the only time in California history when a shore battery engaged in battle with enemy ships, and the only time when its capital, Monterey, fell to a foreign attack. The story of the raids is a story of the struggle of the Spanish-American insurgents to secede from Spain and the desperate efforts by the established order to retain possession of this rich, mission-laden province.

Acknowledgments

First and foremost, I thank Pablo E. Arguindeguy, an Argentine naval historian, for facilitating my access to Argentine archives and providing extensive references about Bouchard.

I am also greatly indebted to the following experts from California for critiquing the manuscript and making many important suggestions:

Edna Kimbro, Architectural Historian and Conservator, Monterey;

John Middleton, Naval Historian, Monterey;

Steven Payne, Assistant Provost, Defense Language Institute, Presidio of Monterey;

Louis Segal, visiting History Lecturer, University of California, Berkeley; and

Robert Senkewicz, Professor of History, Santa Clara University.

The staffs at the Bancroft Library in Berkeley, the Monterey Colton Museum, the Monterey and Santa Cruz public libraries, and the Departamento de Estudios Históricos Navales de la Armada Argentina in Buenos Aires have been most helpful. Their competence and enthusiasm were remarkable.

Several friends helped by editing the manuscript and providing moral support. They include Xavier Maruyama, Evelyn Miller, Fred Snively, Franz and Helga Spickhoff, and Douglas Wilkins. Special thanks to my daughters, Christine, Karen and Jenny Uhrowczik, and my sister, Livia Muruzeta, who contributed both, editing and research. Daily support came from my wife, Theodora, who in her role as a cheerful on-site editor and adviser made this book possible.

I thank them all for their contributions.

I. California as a Colony

Introduction

On a mild November day, after weeks of searching the horizon for a sign of pirates, the lookout at Point Pinos in Monterey[1] saw two ships approaching. Two years before, in 1816, one of the few vessels that sailed to this remote spot had brought news of attacks by Buenos Aires rebels against the Spanish colonies on the Pacific coast of South America. And just a few weeks before the sighting, word had traveled to Monterey that two ships in Hawaii were getting ready to attack Alta California. The lookout raced to spread the news that the feared pirates had arrived. This was the beginning of one of the most important events in the history of Spanish Alta California.

The main actors in this drama were Hipólito Bouchard, a French seaman at the service of the Provincias Unidas del Río de la Plata,[2] (also called Argentina) and Don Pablo Vicente de Solá, the last Spanish governor of Alta California, who resided in Monterey, its capital. Bouchard's story is one of the rough and colorful profession of privateering. Solá's story is one of unbending allegiance to his king in a forbidding and almost abandoned place.

The Wars of Spanish American Independence

The time was 1818, before Mexico ruled Alta California, and long before the United States took over Alta California from Mexico. It was a time when the colors of royal Spain flew over the Province of Alta California. It was also a time when the vast Spanish-American empire, older and much larger than the Anglo-American possessions had ever been, was fading under the siege of Spanish-American insurgents.

The Spanish-American colonies had much the same reasons as the Anglo-American colonies had for seeking independence. The opportunity to revolt came in 1808, when Napoleon inflicted the ultimate affront on Spain by dethroning its king, Fernando VII, and installing his brother Joseph as Spain's monarch. The colonies, realizing that Spain was in disarray, started to rebel. It would take almost twenty years of fierce struggle before most of the Spanish-American colonies were finally freed of Spanish rule. The raid on Alta California took place in the middle of this revolutionary period.

Alta California was a province of New Spain, one of the four viceroyalties that comprised the Spanish-American colonies (the other three were New Granada, Peru and Río de la Plata).

The insurgency in New Spain started in 1810 in today's Mexico. Miguel Hidalgo, a Catholic priest, led a revolt of Indians and poor *mestizos*. It was a social revolution, a revolt as much against Spain as against the affluent Creoles—the Spaniards born in America. By 1810, Hidalgo had been captured, found guilty and shot and his head put on display in a metal cage on the corner of the granary of Guanajuato. The grizzly display remained there for a decade, until Mexico won its inde-

Spanish America before the wars of independence, ca. 1800.

pendence. José María Morelos, another Catholic priest, took up the banner next, but after four years of struggle, he too was executed. Thereafter, the insurgents in Mexico fought a guerrilla war against the royal forces. But the Mexican insurgents never came to Alta California.

Unlike the insurgency in Mexico, the insurgency against Spain in South America was started and supported by well-to-do Creoles. Simón Bolívar in the north and José de San Martín in the south, both gifted leaders, fought for the liberation of South America. By 1816, the Viceroyalty of Río de la Plata, the home of San Martín, had become the independent Provincias Unidas del Río de la Plata. In 1817, in a spectacular military campaign, San Martín led his army from Argentina across the Andes to defeat the Spaniards in the battle of Chacabuco. This victory helped Chile to proclaim its independence. In the same year Bolívar landed with an army in Venezuela and started a series of epic battles pushing westward. By 1818, the war against Spain was at its most intense and was being fought ferociously on land and sea.

Alta California in 1818

Spain's last effort to establish a settlement in the New World was the colonization of Alta California, which took place in 1769.[3] The Spanish period lasted until 1821, when the Mexican rebellion ended Spanish rule in the Viceroyalty of New Spain. Alta California remained under Mexican rule until 1848, when it became part of the United States of America.

Spain had always considered Alta California to be a remote, inaccessible place, difficult to supply and hard to defend. Worst of all, it contained no riches. The decision to colonize it at all was based upon the fear of Russian encroachments. Starting in the first half of the eighteenth century, the Russians had constantly expanded their fur-hunting activities on the western shores of North America. To stop these aggressive intruders, Spain needed a self-sufficient frontier outpost. Spain used its proven method for establishing settlements: it created, with a minimum investment, a chain of missions, presidios, and *pueblos*, which endured thanks to the legendary Spanish bravery, unquestioning allegiance to king, and belief in the Catholic Church. This approach had served Spain well, allowing it— a small country—to control enormous territories throughout the Americas.

In 1818, Alta California was a remote outpost of a failing Spanish-American empire. It consisted of twenty missions, four presidios, and three *pueblos*, scattered over a strip 30 miles wide by 500 miles long, extending from San Diego in the south to San Rafael in the north. Supplies, other than food and basic clothing, came from the port of San Blas in today's state of Nayarit in Mexico, more than 1,500 miles away. Unfavorable winds and currents made this an almost three-month voyage by sea.[4] Access by land had been abandoned after the 1780 massacre of missionaries, settlers, and soldiers by the Yuma Indians on the Colorado River.

Alta California's armed forces consisted of Spanish officers and *mestizo* soldiers reporting to four presidios: Monterey, San Diego, San Francisco, and Santa Barbara. Their task was to protect the twenty missions from Indians and Alta California from foreigners.

Alta California settlements in 1818. Redrawn from *Historical Atlas of California,* Warren A. Beck and Ynez D. Haase. Copyright © 1974 by the University of Oklahoma Press. Reprinted by permission.

The Population

The coast of Alta California was populated by a few Spaniards (Franciscan missionaries and military officers), about 3,000 *mestizos*, and some 20,000 neophytes (converted Indians), who worked at the missions. The Spaniards and the *mestizos* were also called *gente de razón*—literally, people with the ability to reason.

Before the arrival of the Spanish, Alta California was the most densely populated area of what is now the United States.[5] It was home to approximately 300,000 Indians, most of whom lived outside of what would become the coastal mission system. Their population was spread among approximately 500 autonomous tribes of a few hundred individuals each, speaking some 100 mutually unintelligible languages.[6] The isolation and fertility of the land allowed them to live as hunters and gatherers.

The Spanish colonies had a constant need for cheap labor, and the numerous Alta California Indians met this need. From their visitors, the Indians received Christianity, discipline, skills, and diseases. However, they often saw the European concepts of work and discipline as foreign and unnecessary. "We are free! We do not want to obey! We do not want to work!" some of them would say to those who tried to get them to work the land after they were freed, in 1834, by the Mexican government's secularization of the missions.[7]

Spain had difficulty attracting new settlers to Alta California. Unlike England, Spain did not make it easy for settlers to acquire land. During Alta California's Spanish period, no outright land grants were issued to individuals—only provisional

concessions to fewer than thirty retired soldiers.[8] The population growth of the *gente de razón* was primarily the result of the
initial migrations from Mexico and Spain, the intermarriage of
soldiers and Indians, and the sending of some petty criminals
from Mexico to populate the *pueblos*.

The *gente de razón* were mostly illiterate. The few who could
read, read little but the Catechism. In spite of the hard work
necessary to manage their farms and ranches, they remained
extremely generous and hospitable to visitors. Their lives re-
volved around family, church, and music. This culture would
not change until much later, when the arrival of the Anglo-
Americans and other foreigners, brought different priorities.
Meanwhile, as an early governor and enthusiast of Alta California said, "To live long and carefree come to Monterey."[9]

The Missions

There were no rich Creoles in Alta California as there were in
the rest of Spanish America—all of the wealth belonged to the
missions. The mission was the strongest institution in the province followed by the presidio. The *pueblo* was at the bottom of
the pecking order. They were looked down upon by the missions, both because of the unrestrained behavior of their residents[10] and because they were encroaching onto the land that
the missionaries were guarding for the Indians. Relations were
especially strained between the *Pueblo* of Branciforte (today's
Santa Cruz) and the Mission of Santa Cruz.

The explicit purpose of the missions was to save the Indians' souls, to teach them, to protect them, and to prepare them
for assimilation into Spanish society. In theory, the missionar-

ies held the land in trust for the Indians and after ten years were to return it to them. In Alta California, as elsewhere in New Spain, the missionaries argued that ten years was too short a time for the California Indians to become Hispanicized. As a result, the Indians never got their land back. Nevertheless, while the land was under the control of the missionaries, it was safe from the land-grabbers.[11]

Establishing a mission usually required two priests, five soldiers, and hundreds of Indians. Of the twenty missions that existed in Alta California in 1818, the smallest was the Mission at Carmel, with fewer than 400 Indians. The largest was the Mission at San Luis Obispo, with about 2600 Indians.[12] Overall, the twenty missions constituted a prosperous system. They owned some 151,000 head of cattle, 186,000 sheep, and 23,000 horses and produced 76,000 bushels of wheat and 25,000 bushels of corn a year.[13] The missions even managed to provide 400,000 pesos worth of produce to the military, "for which they had received nothing and were not likely to obtain anything" as the Franciscan biographer Zephyrin Engelhardt pointed out.[14]

Horses became so numerous that, in some areas, the governor had to order them slaughtered to keep their numbers down. The settlers became highly dependent on them. "Horses are as abundant here as dogs and chickens," remarked an American visitor. "There are no stables to keep them in, but they are allowed to run wild and graze wherever they please. . . The men usually catch one in the morning, throw a saddle and bridle upon him, and use him for the day, let him go at night, catching another the next day."[15]

Much has been said, both for and against the missionaries' treatment of the Indians. For example, although La Pérouse, a

French explorer who visited Monterey in 1786, praised some of the missionaries, he criticized the harsh subjugation of the natives.[16] It must be remembered, however, that while the Indians did suffer under Spanish and Mexican rule, their condition became worse after the United States occupation.

Hard Times

Alta California was a typical colonial economy in a mercantilist system. It produced raw materials, hides, and tallow, and purchased everything else from the mother country. The settlers were totally dependent on trade with Spanish ships. They were not allowed to trade with vessels from other countries.

Around 1810, California, once thought to be an island, became in effect an economic island. Its primary links to civilization—the annual supply ship from San Blas and the trading ships from Peru—came less and less frequently. The culprits were the nascent Mexican insurrection, the privateers roaming the Pacific coast on behalf of the South American insurgents, and the closing of the land route across Yuma. As a result, neither manufactured goods nor the gold to pay the presidio troops were arriving. The soldiers' morale was low, and they felt bitter about the lack of help from the missionaries. "They had been living on corn for years without ever seeing bread," wrote a visitor to Alta California in 1816, adding that Governor Solá's efforts to curb smuggling prevented them from being supplied with even the barest necessities.[17]

Nevertheless, there was smuggling. The usually loyal administrators and missionaries were increasingly breaking the law and trading with non-Spanish ships.[18] At the same time,

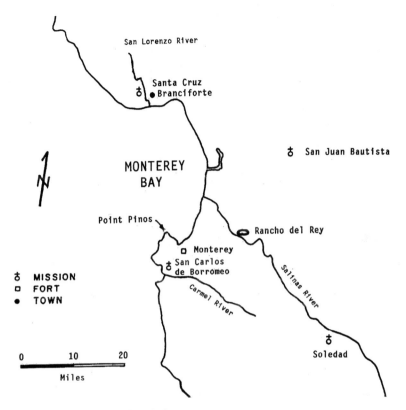

The Monterey Bay area in 1818.

they remained fiercely loyal to the Spanish king, Fernando VII, who had been restored to his throne after Napoleon's fall.

Monterey

In 1818, Monterey, the capital of Alta California and its only official port of entry, was a small and sleepy village. It had a population of about 400, and boasted three main structures: the Royal Presidio of Monterey,[19] a fort called El Castillo de Monterey, and a warehouse by the beach—a precursor of today's Custom House.

21

About thirteen miles northeast lay the Rancho del Rey (part of present-day Salinas). This ranch provided meat and horses for the presidio soldiers and their families.[20] Mission San Carlos de Borromeo, the headquarters of the Alta California mission system, was located four miles south of the Royal Presidio.

Almost the entire population of Monterey lived within the safety of the presidio walls. The presidio was set near the present-day lake El Estero, on Fremont and Church Streets. Peter Corney, who visited Monterey in 1815, estimated the whole population to be "no more than 400 souls." The town, he wrote, had fifty houses and "many farm houses scattered over the plain, with large herds of cattle and sheep."[21] Only one adobe house, built in 1817, existed outside of the presidio. The house was built about one hundred yards south of the presidio by Manuel Boronda, a retired corporal from San Francisco who was a schoolteacher at Monterey and a sacristan.[22]

The Royal Presidio, the community that housed the area residents, seems to have been a square measuring 385 feet on a side.[23] It contained adobe buildings (the "fifty houses" mentioned by Corney) with an enclosed courtyard and was surrounded by an eighteen feet high defensive wall. The adobe buildings included a chapel; the houses of the governor, military officers, married soldiers, and settlers; infantry barracks; smithies; the padres' quarters; a jail, and the royal warehouse.[24] The most imposing building in the presidio was the Royal Presidio Chapel, today's San Carlos Cathedral.

The entire military force of Alta California, including officers, veteran artillerymen, and retired soldiers, consisted of 410 men. This force cost the Spanish government 89,000 pesos per year, "an expense rendered much less burdensome by the fact

Soldier of Monterey, by José Cardero, 1791. Courtesy of the Bancroft
Library, University of California, Berkeley.

that it was never paid."[25]

Of these 410 military men, the Presidio of Monterey hosted approximately 90 with the remainder scattered among the other three presidios.[26] The commander of the Monterey Presidio was also responsible for the safety of six missions: San Carlos, San Antonio, San Luis Obispo, Soledad, San Miguel, and San Juan Bautista.[27] The soldiers assigned to protect them lived at the missions themselves—some 25 men along with their families. Therefore, the permanent garrison stationed at Monterey was about 65 men.

To defend against foreign aggressors, Spain decided to build naval batteries near the four presidios. In times past, Spain

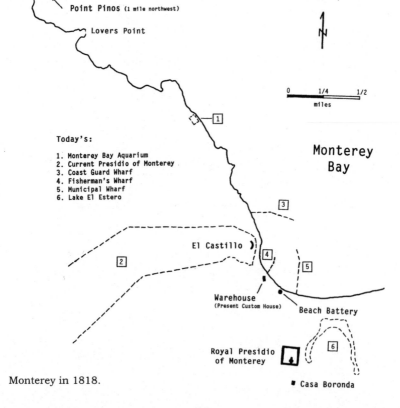

Point Pinos (1 mile northwest)

Lovers Point

N

0   1/4   1/2
miles

Monterey Bay

Today's:

1. Monterey Bay Aquarium
2. Current Presidio of Monterey
3. Coast Guard Wharf
4. Fisherman's Wharf
5. Municipal Wharf
6. Lake El Estero

El Castillo

Warehouse
(Present Custom House)

Beach Battery

Royal Presidio
of Monterey

Monterey in 1818.

Casa Boronda

had built magnificent fortifications, such as St. Augustine in Florida. But now, with its diminishing resources spread thin, Spain was able to build only modest defenses, such as the earthwork fortification built at Monterey at the end of the eighteenth century. Commenting on this fort in 1804, William Shaler,

The Presidio and Pueblo of Monterey, Upper California, watercolor by William Smyth, 1827. The scattered adobe houses did not exist at the time of Bouchard's raid. Courtesy of the Bancroft Library, University of California, Berkeley.

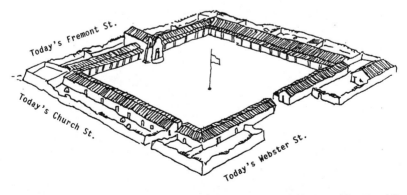

Conjectural view of the Royal Presidio of Monterey, ca. 1820. From The *Presidio of San Carlos de Monterey* . . . Williams, Jack S., 1993. Courtesy of the Center for Spanish Colonial Archeology, San Diego. Today's surrounding streets were added for clarity.

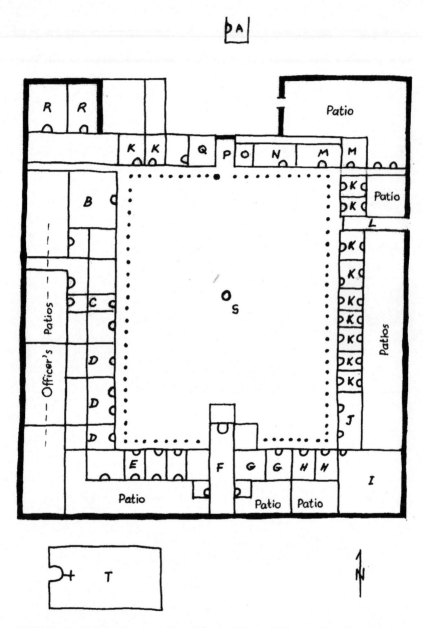

Vallejo's plan of the Monterey Presidio, by Edward Wischer from information obtained from Mariano G. Vallejo, ca. 1878. Redrawn from *The Presidio of San Carlos de Monterey* . . . Williams, Jack S., 1993. Courtesy of the Center for Spanish Colonial Archeology, San Diego.

Today's San Carlos Cathedral, originally the Royal Presidio Chapel. Founded in 1770, the present church structure was completed in 1794. Permission to reproduce from the Diocese of Monetery.

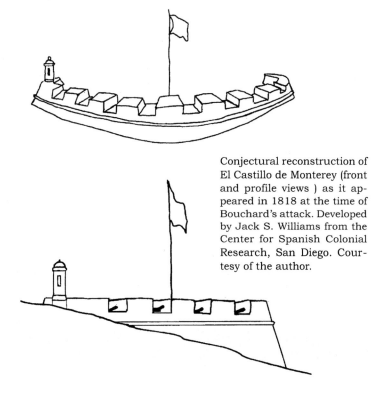

Conjectural reconstruction of El Castillo de Monterey (front and profile views) as it appeared in 1818 at the time of Bouchard's attack. Developed by Jack S. Williams from the Center for Spanish Colonial Research, San Diego. Courtesy of the author.

El Castillo de Monterey, ca. 1833, during the Mexican rule, by Olof Dahlstrand, 1984. The Custom House is in the background by the beach. Farther away is the Royal Presidio with its chapel. Courtesy of the author.

an American sailor, wrote, "There is a miserable battery on a hill that commands the anchorage, but it is altogether inadequate to what it is intended for."[28] By 1816, however, governor Solá had received news about the raids by insurgents on the coasts of South America and was also well aware of the Russian push southwards. In 1817, the fort was reconstructed into a semi-circular battery faced with fired bricks. This battery would enjoy a great distinction—it would become the only fort in California's history to engage in a gun battle with enemy ships.

The fortification at Monterey lay on a hill overlooking the anchoring point for ships. Called, somewhat generously, "El Castillo de Monterey," the approximately 100 feet long structure lay some 200 feet above the beach. The fort had eight cannons and a barracks for the artillerymen.[29] Although the guns could protect against ships coming within its limited range, the fort was vulnerable if the enemy chose to make a remote landing and attack the open fortification from behind.

El Castillo's guns also played a peaceful role. During dense fog, the few ships that entered Monterey fired cannon shots and were guided in by responding El Castillo guns.[30] The fort also participated in the customary ceremonial gun salutes. Describing his visit in 1814 Peter Corney wrote, "I went on shore to report the ship . . . I asked the governor if he would answer a salute; he complied and I went on board and saluted with eleven guns, which was returned."[31]

The Governor: Pablo Vicente de Solá

From 1814 to 1822, the governor of Alta California was Lieutenant Colonel Don Pablo Vicente de Solá—the tenth and last governor of the Spanish colonial era. Like the governors who preceded him, Solá was a military man. A Californian of the time remembers him as "a Spaniard of hidalgo [aristocrat] birth, noble on all four sides—an expression which was in vogue in Spain in the old days to indicate that the individual in question was of hidalgo blood on both his father's and his mother's side."[32] Born in 1761 in the Basque Country of Spain, Solá was better educated than any of his predecessors. He had another high qualification—in 1810, as a captain, he had helped put down the Mexican rebellion led by Father Miguel Hidalgo.[33] Named governor of Alta California in 1814 at age fifty-four, Solá traveled the 1,500 miles from the port of San Blas to Monterey in a voyage that lasted almost three months. This experience, no doubt, convinced him not to expect timely help in case of trouble.

Although no known portrait of Solá exists, he has been described as a man of medium height, with a large head, abundant white hair and beard, and few teeth (this last being not unusual in the early nineteenth century). His voice was measured and his manners affable. He appears to have been a complex man—despotic, quick-tempered, occasionally striking his subordinates, but at the same time impartial, just, amiable, peaceful, and humane. A lifelong bachelor with polished manners, he clearly felt misplaced in this remote place, frequently asking for a better position.[34]

Solá was keenly interested in education. Alta California had almost no schools before his arrival, but by 1818, all four of the presidios and two of the *pueblos* had primary schools taught by settlers and retired soldiers.[35] Solá even suggested that a school be established to educate five or six chosen neophytes from each mission. Solá's liberal attitude was similar to that of La Pérouse, who had mused that instead of being treated like children, the Indians should be given economic opportunities and encouragement so they would truly embrace a new way of life.[36] However, neither the government of New Spain nor the Alta California friars showed much interest.

The province had been hoping for a strong, pro-monarchy leader. When Solá arrived, the people welcomed him with three days of celebrations to a degree never seen before.[37] Everyone of importance in Alta California was there and the eyewitnesses remembered the occasion many decades later. Evergreens and extra lights decorated the presidio enclosure, and on the flagpole floated the beloved colors of Spain. The events started with a High Mass at the presidio church. Three dozen Indians dressed in bright colors accompanied the friar's chants with musical instruments while muskets and cannons cracked outside. Next, Solá delivered a speech to the troops, including the cavalry who stood in parade formation, dressed in their traditional cueras (protective many-layered buckskin vests and pants). He praised everyone, to the shouts "Long live the king!" "Long live the governor!" and "Long live the father missionaries!" A banquet and a fight between a bull and a grizzly bear—a common Californian entertainment—followed, and the long day ended with an all-night dance. The following morning another High Mass was held, this time at the Mission of San Carlos. After the Mass, the painted and adorned Indians engaged in a mock battle among themselves and later deposited their arms at the feet of the governor.

Once the festivities were over, Solá assessed the condition of the province and reported to the viceroy of New Spain that Alta California was not capable of repelling an external attack. The Russians, who as recently as 1812 had established Fort Ross to increase their fur hunting and fur trade, could not be expelled. As gold was to the Spaniards, so fur was to the shrewd Russians. They focused on hunting sea otter, whose pelts were extremely valuable. They even brought expert sea otter hunters, Kodiak Indians from their settlement in Sitka, Alaska, to help them. Solá repeatedly asked the Russians to leave, but they, being superior in strength, ignored him. This conflict, however, did not stop the Spaniards from trading with the Russians even when lacking the permission from the viceroy to do so.[38]

What he really needed, Solá wrote prophetically to the viceroy, were not expensive fortifications, which would be useless, but 200 infantrymen, four guns with skilled artillerymen, and an armed cruiser.[39] So began a long series of bitter complaints to the viceroy about the lack of resources in this lonely outpost. Solá lamented that his troops were not fit to fight against an enemy armed with anything more than bows and arrows. A perceptive man, Solá distrusted the Anglo-Americans, who, through frequent visits to the coast, had learned of the province's riches—and of its defenseless condition. Surely, he thought, the Anglo-Americans were interested in more than just trading and smuggling.[40]

The Alarm

In 1816, chilling news came from South America—the ports of Callao (Peru) and Guayaquil (Ecuador) were being raided by insurgents from Buenos Aires. One of the raiders was Captain Hipólito Bouchard. But this was not part of the news, and even if it had been, it would have meant nothing to the Californians at that time.

The worried Solá immediately sent instructions to the presidios and missions—place sharp lookouts on the coast, use the least valuable paper archives to make cartridges, and be prepared at a moment's notice to gather fifteen to twenty native *vaqueros* (Indian cowboys) from each mission to defend the presidios. Praise the Indians to keep them happy, exhort them to loyalty, and above all, resist to the last drop of blood any insurgent invasion. In other words, do the best with what you've got. The viceroy was equally worried: he sent Solá eight guns of 8 pounds caliber, 100 English muskets, and ammunition. Time passed, and the insurgents did not come.[41]

However, on October 8, 1818 an express messenger from Santa Barbara delivered the bad news to Governor Solá. Two days earlier, the American ship *Clarion* had arrived in Santa Barbara from Hawaii. Her captain, Henry Gyzelaar, had told the commander of Santa Barbara, Don José de la Guerra y Noriega, that two insurgent ships in Hawaii were getting ready to raid the American coast. Gyzelaar was thus paying for the kindness shown to him in the past by his friends, the Noriegas. This unexpected intelligence coup would prove crucial to the defense of Alta California.

Solá immediately sent orders to the presidios and missions similar to those he had sent in 1816. "Under the protection of the God of battles," De la Guerra responded, "I believe I can destroy all such villains as may have the rashness to set foot on this soil."[42] Six weeks went by with no sightings of the insurgents, and the governor started to have second thoughts. Was de la Guerra just an alarmist? Solá even sent him a letter of reprimand. At about the same time, however, the lookout at Point Pinos saw two ships approaching Monterey. Hipólito Bouchard was nearing the California coast.

II. Privateering

Bouchard was a privateer. Privateering was a risky and colorful profession that originated in the Middle Ages and extended through the end of the nineteenth century. To understand Bouchard's raid, one must first understand privateering.

Starting in the sixteenth century, the governments of England, France, Holland, and later the United States, sought to increase their naval power by turning to privateering. A privateer, a mercenary of the sea, was a privately owned vessel and its crew, armed and operated at the owner's expense with a government license to attack and seize enemy ships. In short, privateering was a way to create privately financed navies. The authorization to attack the enemy was not limited to shipping— land attacks were certainly acceptable. England, anti-Catholic and resentful of Spain's trade monopoly in its American colonies, had commissioned many privateers. Perhaps the most famous was Francis Drake, commissioned in 1577 by Queen Elizabeth I to harass the Spanish on the Pacific coast of the Americas. Those were lucrative times for privateers, preying on the richly loaded Spanish vessels returning from their colonies, many of which fell prey to Drake. In recognition of his services, the Queen bestowed knighthood upon Drake.

During the early nineteenth century, privateering was a legal, respected, and even admired profession. Technically, the difference between a pirate and a privateer was a piece of paper—a letter of marque and instructions issued by a government that specified against whom and for how long the privateering was to be done. The ship was owned and equipped by one or more investors, the shipowners, who would contract a captain to embark on a privateering voyage. To guarantee that the privateer would follow the instructions, the shipowner had to deposit a security bond with the government issuing the letter of marque. Privateers would stop any ship, examine its papers, and, if they found it to be at the service of the declared enemy, seize it. This would, technically, make the prey a prize.

For a privateer, if there were no captured prizes, there was no income. The prize had to be hauled back home, where an admiralty court would determine whether it had been legitimately seized. If the court condemned the prize—that is, determined that the ship had indeed been serving the enemy—the prize was sold and the proceeds parceled out. This unique reward system explains some of the excesses attributed to privateers—unlike their counterparts in regular navies, they had to get prizes to make a living. The impunity provided by the wide oceans and poor communications increased the temptation to make a profit. Common excesses included sacking ships that were not at the service of the enemy or using the letters of marque beyond the authorization date. The financial rewards were large and the profession attracted men who loved risk and adventure. Privateering was so successful that England, for example, had trouble attracting crews into its own growing regular navy. The reasons were both the harsh treatment of sailors in England's navy as well as the potential to make more money as privateers.

The fledging United States government used privateers during its Revolutionary War and even more extensively during the War of 1812, when approximately 500 privateers captured up to 1,700 English vessels.[1] Baltimore was one of the most active ports, outfitting many of the ships and crews. Privateering was a profitable business, with a system of investors, shipbuilders, regulations, and even a Privateer's Fund providing pensions.[2] Investors ranged from merchants to judges to postmasters.

After 1814, when the United States and Great Britain signed the peace treaty, Baltimore's privateering business hit a slump. Luckily for the entrepreneurs, the South American struggle against Spain was at its peak. Although the United States government was neutral during the Spanish-American Revolution, its privateering business with its idle ships and crews was available to the insurgents. Sometimes ships were sold directly to the insurgents; at other times, captains with their own ships and experienced crews headed south to offer their services. Many letters of marque were also sold directly in the United States. Of the 225 letters issued by Buenos Aires, about 100 are listed as "blank." These letters were probably bought, legally and illegally, by U. S. agents for resale in the United States.[3]

Governments, of course, wanted to do as much damage as possible to their enemies, and the more privateers they could authorize, the better. The shipowners and the privateers wanted to make money, but they needed the letters of marque—from any country that was issuing them. Of the thirty-six Buenos Aires privateers operating in the Atlantic in 1818-1819, at least twenty were United States ships and some of them never knew the country that provided them with the letters of marque.[4] The privateers operated off Cuba, Puerto Rico, the Canary Islands, and even peninsular Spanish ports such as Cádiz, inflicting a severe blow on Spanish commerce. As an example, Captain Almeida, a Portuguese American at the service of the Buenos Aires insurgents, inspected 167 vessels on the open sea and found that 24 were enemy ships.[5] He burned 5, returned 9, and sent 7 to Buenos Aires and 3 to the United States.

Approximately 3,500 American sailors worked on the South American raiders between 1816 and 1821.[6] This situation was too much for Spain. Its minister to the United States complained bitterly about this to Secretary of State John Quincy Adams.[7] The minister even used the interest of the United States in the purchase of Florida from Spain as a negotiating card to rein in the privateers.[8] While the people of the United States were sympathetic to the insurgency against Spain, the United States government did not formally recognize the rebels and applied pressure on the insurgents and their privateering activities.[9] It was not until 1821—with Spain almost totally defeated in the Americas—that Buenos Aires reined in its privateers. Two years later, the United States issued the famous Monroe doctrine, declaring the "Americas for Americans," thus implicitly recognizing the Spanish-American struggle for independence. At this point, the privateering against Spain had the blessing of the United States, but by then it was almost over anyway.

The Privateer: Hipólito Bouchard

Hipólito Bouchard was the most colorful privateer at the service of the rebels from Buenos Aires. He was baptized André

Paul, but later in life changed his name to Hypolite (French) or Hipólito (Spanish).[10] This was also his younger brother's name, a fact that creates confusion for historians. André Paul was born in the Provence region of southern France on January 15, 1780. He served in Napoleon's navy during the Egyptian campaign—showing bravery—and later participated in an expedition to Haiti.[11] He left France for the United States and came ashore in Buenos Aires around 1810.[12] Unlike many other privateers at the service of Buenos Aires, who were in it just for the money, Bouchard adapted Argentina as his second home, married a local lady, fought in the Spanish-American wars of independence, and became an officer in the Argentine army and navy.

Bouchard's first biographer, Bartolomé Mitre, described him as a tall man of dark complexion, with black, piercing eyes, an energetic stride, and the confident air of someone accustomed to lead.[13] As for his formal education, "judging by his letters, Bouchard had very limited culture."[14] A Chilean historian, Barros Arana, left the following sketch of Bouchard:

> French adventurer . . . had acquired fame for bravery during his land and sea services under the Argentine flag. Fearless to the point of recklessness, arrogant and excitable, rough in manners, without culture and hard in his feelings.[15]

Teodoro Caillet-Bois, an Argentine historian, agreed with this description, "It is a very precise portrait," he wrote.[16]

Why did Bouchard, as well as other Frenchmen, join the insurgents of Buenos Aires? As one of his compatriots, Luis

Santiago Scoffier, wrote:

> After the fall of Napoleon and the subsequent perse-
> cutions by the new monarch, and because of my lib-
> eral principles, I decided to avoid them and emigrate
> to a free country like Buenos Aires with the purpose
> to serve and contribute to the destruction of the tyr-
> anny and the consolidation of this independent Re-
> public, for which reason I abandoned the ship that
> brought me.[17]

However, Scoffier came to Buenos Aires after the fall of Napoleon, while Bouchard came when the victorious Napoleon
was still in power. Why he emigrated at that time remains unknown.

In the year 1818, the newly independent Provincias Unidas
del Río de la Plata was a prosperous country. Situated at the
convergence of the wide Río de la Plata and the Atlantic Ocean,
Buenos Aires, its capital, had a population of more than 40,000,
of whom 70 percent were white, 25 percent black, 3 percent
mestizo and 2 percent Indian, a decidedly European city.[18]
Buenos Aires had always rebelled against its colonial masters,
especially against the laws forcing it to trade only with Spain.
According to the Spaniards, Buenos Aires was a smugglers'
nest, but it was a free trade heaven according to the natives.

Great Britain also coveted the riches of this vast and fertile
land, known as the Viceroyalty of Río de la Plata. In the early
1800s, Britain had sent two military expeditions to "liberate"
this land from Spain. Both invasions were defeated with strong
help from the local population. Later, however, the inhabitants

turned against their Spanish masters, and became an independent country in 1816.

Between 1815 and 1821, proud of their successes, the Buenos Aires insurgents saw an opportunity to hasten Spain's defeat by attacking its exposed military supply and commercial trade lines. They relied on privateers while they started to form their own navy using foreign soldiers of fortune.

The early navy of the Buenos Aires rebels consisted of three ships commanded by Frenchmen—Juan Bautista Azopardo, Angel Hubac, and Bouchard. In 1811 they saw their first action, suffering defeat at the hands of the more experienced Spanish naval force. During the same year, the Spanish navy repeatedly attacked Buenos Aires and Bouchard distinguished himself for bravery. As the naval activities around Buenos Aires decreased, the fledgling navy was disbanded, leaving Bouchard without a job.[19]

In 1812, José de San Martín, the future liberator of Chile, established what would become an Argentine elite unit—the Escuadrón de Granaderos a Caballo (mounted grenadiers). Bouchard, a budding revolutionary, joined the group as an officer.[20] Now on horseback, he was recognized by San Martín for bravery in the battle of San Lorenzo, where he seized the enemy's flag and killed the flagbearer.[21]

By his third year in Buenos Aires, Bouchard had put down roots in his adopted country. He was granted citizenship, was promoted to a captain, and married Doña Norberta Merlo, the daughter of a prominent local family.

In the unstable political climate of the Province Unidas, Bouchard was so indiscreet, as a confidential memo relates, to "express subversive ideas, spread false news and attempt to undermine the government."[22] As this account will show, Bouchard's personality was not suited for sophisticated conspiracies. Most likely his problems were caused by his own directness. At one point, one of his letters—critical of the supreme director of the Provincias Unidas—was intercepted. As a result, Bouchard wrote, "I saved my life but I lost my military post . . . my squadron was given to someone else, to my dishonor. This ugly event prompted me to seek the enemy at sea." His superiors agreed, saying, "at sea he may be of better value to the country."[23]

While Bouchard was a grenadier, the government made another attempt to form a navy. Command was given to Guillermo Brown, a congenial and capable Irishman who would become Argentina's most distinguished sailor.[24] Although Bouchard was an experienced seaman, he was not called upon to help. Was it because Bouchard was French and Brown was Irish? We do not know.

Brown's squadron achieved brilliant victories in the Río de la Plata, to the point that there was, again, little need for a standing government navy; and so the squadron was disarmed.

The desire to liberate the Americas from Spanish colonial rule was very strong among the insurgents from Buenos Aires. Brown now got interested in an idea San Martín had—to harass the Spaniards along the Pacific coast of South America and promote the idea of insurrection against Spain while San Martín was preparing his army to attack the Spaniards in Chile and Peru.[25]

To reduce costs, the government designated Brown and his two ships as privateers. Bouchard now saw his opportunity to return to sea service. He too obtained a privateer's commission and in October 1815, at the head of the corvette *Halcón*, joined the group under Brown's command. This was the start of Bouchard's career as a privateering captain at the service of the Buenos Aires government.

The First Voyage

Commanding a privateering ship was not for the weak of heart. Several incidents during the campaign show how rough life was on a privateering ship. At one point Bouchard's officers, tired of the difficult voyage around Cape Horn, demanded to capture a ship—any ship, sell her at the first stop, and each go his own way with the proceeds. Bouchard resisted with the help of a Chilean officer who gave the enterprising crew a tough choice: either continue the cruise or be dispatched to heaven.[26] Bouchard won at the price of a sour contingent—"They even tried to poison me," he wrote.[27] Things got even tougher when, after capturing the schooner *Andaluz,* Bouchard physically mistreated her captain and accused his own officers (who in turn accused him) of stealing some of the captured goods.[28]

In a daring move, the insurgents blockaded the port of Callao, Peru, and captured several vessels, including the Spanish frigate *Consecuencia*. Two years later, the *Consecuencia* became the notorious *La Argentina*,[29] one of the two vessels to come to Monterey. The prisoners included the governor of the Spanish Guayaquil (present-day Ecuador).[30]

The next target was Guayaquil, where the Spaniards took the popular Brown as prisoner. For some reason—perhaps due to a growing mutual dislike between the two men—Bouchard was reluctant to help rescue the popular Irishman. Bouchard's

Hipólito Bouchard, oil by José Gil de Castro, 1819. Courtesy of the Departamento de Estudios Históricos Navales de la Armada Argentina, Buenos Aires.

officers disagreed—one brandishing a pistol—and Brown was exchanged for the prisoners, including the valuable governor of Guayaquil, along with some of the prizes taken in Callao.[31] Loosing the hard-earned prizes was not to Bouchard's liking, and from this point on, the relations between the two privateers worsened. It was time for each to go his own way. The two men agreed on how to split the prizes; Bouchard got the *Consecuencia* and returned to Buenos Aires.

The voyage had left hard feelings among Bouchard and his crew. The stormy captain lost no time in accusing some of his officers of insubordination. They, in turn, filed counter-charges.[32] Bouchard was absolved but the incident left him with enemies and before long an unknown man attacked him with a knife. Not one to avoid a fight, Bouchard stabbed the attacker. Later, he commented that the man had probably been sent by Luis Scoffier, a disgruntled officer from his recent Pacific campaign.[33]

The campaign along the Pacific coast was a political and military success. The privateers disrupted Spanish commerce, heralding the rebellion against Spain. As a result, the Spanish governments along the Pacific coast went into panic. The disturbing news about the rebel raids also reached Governor Solá in Alta California. The campaign was also a financial success. One record shows that for the Bouchard portion of the expedition, an investment of 45,441 pesos realized a profit of 60,084 pesos; this profit was divided equally among the shipowners, the officers, and the crew.[34]

By now, Bouchard had emerged as a quick-tempered man of action—brave, decisive, and capable of commanding a privateering vessel at a profit—in short, an ideal privateer.

The Chance of a Lifetime

The Provincias Unidas were now at the peak of their privateering attacks on Spain. Between the years 1815 and 1821, Buenos Aires-sponsored privateers captured a total of fifty-four enemy ships. During 1818, the Provincias Unidas had twenty-three active privateers in service.[35] One admirer of the Buenos Aires privateers was Simón Bolívar, who wrote, "Experience has proven the value of privateering, especially in our struggle with Spain. The government of Buenos Aires, who used them most, is also the best known, respected and feared."[36]

Bouchard's next assignment was to command the frigate *La Argentina*, formerly the *Consecuencia*, in a privateering voyage. The ship was now owned by a partnership headed by the Argentine patriot and investor Vicente Anastasio de Echevarría. He admired Bouchard's achievements and made him captain of the highly prized vessel.[37] Just a year before Bouchard had achieved the rank of lieutenant commander.[38]

Carrying 164 men, the 464-ton frigate was armed with thirty-four 8- and 12-caliber guns. She set out to sea on July 9, 1817. It was the first anniversary of the independence of the Provincias Unidas del Río de la Plata.[39]

The departure of *La Argentina* was an important event for this young republic. The country's pride was at its peak. It had defeated two English invasions. It had become independent from Spain. Then, San Martín's efficient army had crossed the Andes to defeat the Spaniards in Chile. And now a large vessel owned by local entrepreneurs, and commanded by a citizen of the Provincias Unidas was about to join the struggle against Spain.

To add to the local pride, all of the officers were dressed in naval uniforms designed just three years before.[40] The officers were mostly foreigners, and their surnames suggest the various countries from which they came—Somers (second in command), Berges, Crassack, Mills, Oliver, Sheppard, Thompson, Douglas, Ahriens and Vamburgen.[41] A few were natives from Río de la Plata, like José María Piriz, the officer commanding the marines who wrote an account of the voyage. Another local was sixteen-year-old Tomás Domingo Espora, who was to become one of Argentina's naval heroes. Espora also served as the scribe for Bouchard's account of *La Argentina*'s voyage. A third local, the fifteen-year-old ship's boy Julián Manrique, also wrote a memoir of the voyage.

The Voyage around the World

Before *La Argentina* set sail, neither the government, Bouchard, nor Echevarría knew that she would be embarking on a long voyage around the world. Such a voyage would have been of no military value to the Provincias Unidas. In fact, it was contrary to the instructions that the government had issued to Anastasio Echevarría, the owner of *La Argentina*. The instructions were issued on June 25, 1817, just two weeks before the ship's departure.[42]

The instructions offered Bouchard a number of options for the voyage: the South Pacific, with a blockade of Lima; the ports of Spain, especially Cádiz, "the most active port in the world"; or the Caribbean and the northeast of South America. Instead, Bouchard ignored all three options and set sail for the Philippines, California and Central America. Who, then, decided that *La Argentina* should go around the world? This remains a mys-

List of officers and supplies of *La Argentina* on its departure from Buenos Aires in 1817. Archivo General de la Nación, Buenos Aires, Legajo X.5.1.5.

Argentine naval uniforms used during the wars of independence against Spain, by Mario Luqui-Lagleyze. During the voyage of *La Argentina*, Bouchard wore the third uniform from the left. Courtesy of the Instituto Nacional Browniano, Buenos Aires.

tery—and neither Bouchard's report of the voyage nor the archives of Anastasio Echevarría shed any light on it. Since the government had not issued the order, Echevarría and Bouchard must have made the decision themselves. But what prompted them to do so?

We know that Bouchard had his eye on the Spanish possession of the Philippines as early as 1816.[43] However, an episode in 1817 raised his interest again. Shortly before *La Argentina* sailed, an important event occurred in the privateering community of Buenos Aires: a United States-owned ship, the *Tupac Amaru,* and her captain, a U.S. citizen, carrying a letter of marque from the Provincias Unidas, captured the *Tritón,* a ship with a value of more than one million dollars that had sailed from the Philippines.[44] This was the highest single prize claimed by the privateers of Buenos Aires during the wars of independence. The *Tritón* arrived in Buenos Aires on April 1, 1817, no doubt impressing the owners and captains of privateering vessels. Since *La Argentina* was getting ready for a privateering voyage, why not go directly to the Philippines and capture these rich ships where they originated? This would mean a trip halfway around the world, but for the brave and impulsive Bouchard such an adventure must have been appealing. As for doing his patriotic duty—well, he would still be capturing Spanish ships and Spanish property.

Coincidentally, on the same day the *Tritón* arrived in Buenos Aires, the triumphant General San Martín paid the town a short visit from the recently liberated Chile. One purpose of the visit was to discuss with the government his plans to attack the Spaniards in Peru, a loyal and powerful Spanish garrison in South America. He wanted to transport his army by sea. To protect it, he needed money to form a squadron of at least five corvettes. Did he, perhaps, hope to get *La Argentina*? A warship the size of *La Argentina* could not have escaped San Martín's attention. He wanted the ships ready in Chile in four months;[45] however, just three months after San Martín's visit, Bouchard sailed in the opposite direction—towards the Philippines. Furthermore, there is no record of any discussions between San Martín and Echevarría or Bouchard. All this suggests that it was highly unlikely that *La Argentina* was designated to be part of San Martín's plans to invade Peru. However, it is highly probable that both Echevarría and Bouchard knew about San Martín's plans before *La Argentina* left Buenos Aires.

A riot marred the departure of *La Argentina*. A drunken sailor slapped an officer and Bouchard ordered his arrest. However, the other sailors had also been drinking; there was a general melee, and Bouchard was attacked with a hatchet, "which he evaded and proceeded to stab the aggressor." The second in command, the Englishman Somers, suppressed the riot with the help of the marines at the cost of two dead and four wounded.[46] This incident provoked concern about the lack of discipline on the ship and an investigation ensued, but while the investigation was still in progress, *La Argentina* sailed. Her sudden departure provoked rumors among Bouchard's enemies that he had exploited Echevarría's trust and "stole the ship to use for his own benefit."[47] Echevarría defended Bouchard's honor by vehemently denying the rumors.[48]

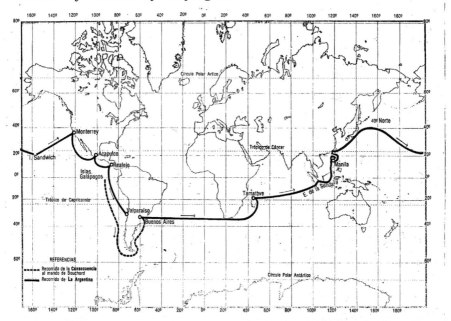

The voyage of *La Argentina* around the world, 1817-1819. Courtesy of the Departamento de Estudios Históricos Navales de la Armada Argentina, Buenos Aires.

The frigate headed for the Cape of Good Hope, and what followed must be considered one of the great adventures in privateering.[49]

Slave Trade

On September 4, 1817, after two months at sea, *La Argentina* reached the port of Toamasina in Madagascar. There, Bouchard noticed four ships engaged in slave trade. At the time, Britain was trying to prevent such trade, and it had an officer posted in the port. This officer asked Bouchard for help while he was waiting for a British corvette to arrive. "I offered him all the forces under my command and said that I would do all I could to prevent such a vile commerce, by virtue of the treaties with the European Nations and the high aims of Your Excellency which are to abolish, within your reach, all forms of slavery," Bouchard wrote to Pueyrredón, the man who had authorized his letter of marque.[50] There is a genuine, almost quixotic, enthusiasm in Bouchard's writing about the incident: he wants to do good, to represent his adopted country well.

Bouchard held the slave ships until the British corvette arrived. Later, the captains of the slave ships filed two protests before the government of the Provincias Unidas. They accused the Bouchard crew of stealing provisions and of behaving like pirates—but Bouchard did give them a note to be paid by the government of Buenos Aires.[51]

Scurvy

By November 1817, four months into the voyage, eighty-four of

Bouchard's crew had developed scurvy. Over forty of these men eventually died.[52] Bouchard stopped for eleven days at an island while he attempted to have them cured. After normal treatment procedures had failed, he directed that the sick be buried up to their necks in holes four feet deep. He reported that "those that were totally infected died within an hour, the rest did improve."[53]

The cure for scurvy, and the means of preventing it, was known at the time of Bouchard's voyage. The British, ever more dependent on their navy, had been trying to solve this problem for most of the eighteenth century. By 1796, the British Royal Navy knew that vitamin C-rich foods were the cure and it issued lemon juice, and vegetables to its sailors. But it was difficult to preserve these foods, and frequent stops to replenish the ship's stores were needed. Obviously, Bouchard, embarked on a long voyage and putting in at unfamiliar ports had not been able to replenish his supply in time.

Pirate Attack

Sailing through the Makassar Strait off the island of Borneo, with its crew still weak from scurvy, *La Argentina* was attacked by pirates on five Malayan proas—swift sailboats with a flat lee side and a single outrigger. After one and half-hours of fighting, Bouchard tells us, the captain of one of the proas, probably seeing that he was about to be taken captive, committed suicide by stabbing himself and jumping into the water. Five men followed his example. *La Argentina*'s crew suffered seven wounded and took forty-two prisoners. Bouchard consulted with his officers about what to do with them. The officers felt that as pirates, the prisoners should be punished, but since most of

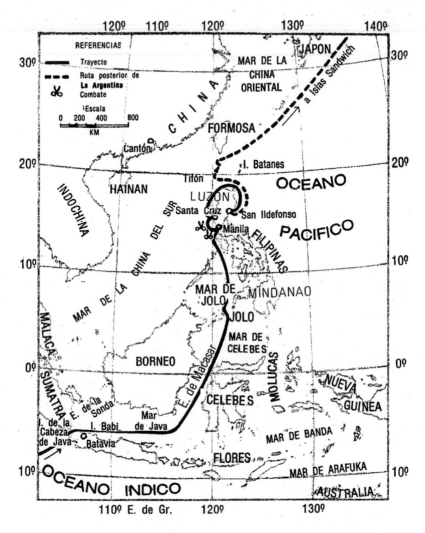

Bouchard in Indonesia and the Philippines. Courtesy of the Departamento de Estudios Históricos Navales de la Armada Argentina, Buenos Aires.

them were wounded, the officers wanted to let them go. Bouchard took a harder line. He kept some of the young prisoners as his own crew, sent the rest back to their proa, and sunk her with the men on board.[54] The remaining proas fled.

Blockade of Manila

In January 1818, six months after his departure, Bouchard reached Manila. For the next two months *La Argentina* cruised in its waters, hoping to catch rich prizes like the *Tritón*. But no such prizes appeared.

Bouchard learned that the port of Manila was hosting two Spanish ships and one war corvette, none of which left port while Bouchard was there. He wrote, "The miserables instead of coming out kept the ships inside and embargoed all commercial ships of the island of Luzon. I cruised for three months in front of them without a single ship daring to leave."[55] All that Bouchard found in the waters of Manila were sixteen small vessels carrying only sugar and rice. From their crews he learned that the troops in Manila were reduced to eating starvation rations of rice. He had all sixteen vessels sunk.

In March 1818, after leaving the waters of Manila, the privateers spotted a brigantine. Trying to escape, the brigantine entered the shallow port of Santa Cruz, where *La Argentina* could not follow. Undaunted, Bouchard sent three boats to board her. A fight ensued and the privateers lost fourteen men—a big loss, for one of them, Nathan Somers, was *La Argentina's* second in command. Eventually they did capture the brigantine and later a schooner as well.[56] The three ships navigated together for a few days, but then the captured vessels disappeared and "up to this date [I have] never heard of them again," lamented Bouchard.[57] The result was a further loss of men—eight men and one officer who had been placed on the schooner. Bouchard suspected the schooner's crew of escaping to Macao or Canton "because of their greed for the silver and other goods that were aboard."

Up to this point, Bouchard's voyage had been filled with misfortune. After almost a year he had seized no prizes, his crew was decimated and sick, he was low on food, and he was 16,000 miles from home. He also learned that because of the upheaval caused by the Mexican revolution, the ships from Acapulco and San Blas no longer came to Manila. This significantly decreased his chance of getting prizes. Furthermore, the Manila Company had stopped transporting silver on its ships. Unfortunately for Bouchard, Spain was almost defeated, and there was little for a privateer to prey on—just the opposite of the rich convoys that Drake had found in the glory days of Spain.

Grimly, Bouchard pondered what to do next. He considered several options. Maybe he should try his luck in Canton. Or perhaps he should go to the island of Saint Helena and liberate Napoleon. Bouchard conceived this surprising idea after he learned about Napoleon's misfortunes from the captain of a French ship. Perhaps he planned to take Napoleon to South America to head the war against Spain. Bouchard's exuberant and impulsive character emerges in these fantasies; "He was tempted for many days to start such a daring enterprise, impossible for all but Bouchard." [58]

Another obvious alternative was to return the same way he had came—not very appealing, since he had not made any friends on his stopovers, and he knew that there were no Spanish prizes along that path route. On the other hand, since he was already halfway around the world from home, he could continue east and sail right around the world. Surely the Spaniards were trying to supply their beleaguered ports on the Pacific coast of America—Callao, Guayaquil, and Acapulco—all of which would provide good opportunities for prizes. Also, as he had learned before departing from Buenos Aires, his former commander, General San Martín, was with his army in Chile trying to liberate Peru.[59] The general could surely use his help.

Bouchard made a last attempt to reverse his fortunes in Asian waters. Learning that the Manila Company had sent three of her ships to China to take on cargo, Bouchard departed on May 21, 1818, to capture them.[60] A storm lasting six days decimated the already-sick sailors, "there were days when up to three died." The deplorable condition of his crew forced Bouchard's hand; he departed for the Hawaiian Islands, which were, then as now, an ideal place to rest body and spirit.

The decision had been made—he would head east, a voyage around the world. With a sickly crew scarcely able to work the ship, *La Argentina* reached Kealakekua Bay on the western shores of the island of Hawaii on August 18, 1818. Here, two events occurred that were to influence Bouchard's next steps. One was the seizure of the corvette *Santa Rosa de Chacabuco*. The other was Bouchard's first meeting with the Englishman Peter Corney.

The *Santa Rosa*

When the privateers arrived at what looked and felt like paradise, Bouchard learned that the king of Hawaii, Kamehameha I, owned a vessel that had once been Spanish. "I didn't know what to do, an armed Spanish vessel in the hands of these barbarians," he wrote. It turned out that the vessel was the Philadelphia-built 280-ton corvette *Santa Rosa de Chacabuco*, which had sailed from Buenos Aires as a Provincias Unidas privateer two months before Bouchard's departure.[61] Her crew had mutinied off the Chilean coast, setting the officers ashore and proceeding to loot ports in Peru and Ecuador. Enriched, they had then headed for Hawaii, where they sold the ship to the king and dispersed to the different islands.

On learning this, Bouchard was furious and determined to take action. He would recover the corvette for the Provincias Unidas, and punish the mutineers according to custom—while giving a strong message to his own crew about what happens to mutineers. He started by negotiating with the king for the return of the vessel. To facilitate the discussions—and convinced that the Provincias Unidas would want him to recover the corvette—he wrote himself an authorization letter from the "Sovereign Congress of the United Provinces of Río de La Plata" stating that he should seize the ship.[62] This did not work with the king, and Bouchard had to pay for the vessel and some of the mutineers, "which cost me more than had I bought them as slaves." Finally, however, the *Santa Rosa* and the mutineers were recovered. One of the leaders, Griffiths, was condemned to death by a war council of Bouchard's officers, but that night "the king himself let him escape." This was more than the determined captain could bear, and he gave the king six hours to return the man. To show that he meant business, he ordered his artillery to get ready and to start heating the cannonballs. The king, realizing that Bouchard might carry out his threat, returned the condemned man. Griffiths was executed on the beach after "getting two hours to reconcile himself with the All Mighty and the duties of his religion." The other mutineers, according to Corney, got twelve dozen lashes, "which tore their backs in a shocking manner."

Meeting Peter Corney

While in Hawaii, Bouchard met Peter Corney, and grew to like him. Judging by Corney's memoirs, he was an alert and perceptive man. He had sailed in 1813 as first lieutenant on the schooner *Columbia*, a ship fitted by English firms for fur trading between the northwest coast of America and China. In the process, he had come to know Hawaii well.

Corney had arrived at Hawaii before Bouchard. He had become suspicious of the *Santa Rosa* crew when he learned that they had sold the corvette to the king for almost nothing. He realized that the crew had mutinied after talking with a "half intoxicated" sailor from the *Santa Rosa*.[63] He had told the story to the king and later, no doubt, to Bouchard.

But the Englishman also knew another story—the story of Monterey.

Very likely it was his encounter with Corney that led to Bouchard's decision to raid Monterey. Corney had visited Monterey just three years earlier. Bouchard had many discussions with the Englishman in the balmy breezes of Hawaii. Corney wrote that, "on their arrival, Captain Bouchard came to our houses, where he spent most of his time, often inviting us on board. He took a particular fancy to me." Thus, Bouchard got fresh information about Monterey, its harbor, its presidio, its garrison, and its suspected riches. One can only speculate that the two discussed the multiple possibilities. Maybe they would find Spanish ships coming to Monterey bringing goods for the province and salaries for the troops. Maybe Monterey, being the capital, had valuables worth looting. Maybe the mestizo population was ready to revolt, and Bouchard and Corney could help them to gain their independence, perhaps even creating a new Spanish-American republic.

By now, Bouchard's situation had greatly improved. He had doubled his small armada, he had a healthy and replenished crew, and above all, he had a plan—to attack Alta California before heading home. Bouchard put Corney at the helm of the *Santa Rosa*, and on October 25, 1818, they sailed for Alta California.

During the voyage, anticipating resistance from the Spaniards, the captains drilled their crews into a fighting force. "On our passage towards California," Corney reported, "we were employed exercising the great guns, and putting the ship in good condition for fighting, frequently reading the articles of war which are very strict, and punish with death almost every act of insubordination."[64]

III. The Raid on California

The Raid on Monterey

Midway through the trip to California a seemingly insignificant event occurred that would come to haunt Bouchard—his letter of marque expired.[1] He must have known that to continue raiding the Spanish would make him technically a pirate. But such details did not deter a man of Bouchard's drive. Had he been able to communicate with the government of Provincias Unidas, no doubt he would have received an extension. So, a pirate by the letter of the law but a privateer in spirit, the determined captain proceeded to Monterey.

On approaching the American coast, the small fleet stopped to get supplies at the Russian port of Bodega Bay, 180 miles north of Monterey.[2] The Russians had visited Monterey just a few months earlier. Despite the fact that the Russians were trading with the Spanish, all the Russians ever heard from the Spaniards officially was that they should pack up and leave. This cool relationship may have made it possible for Bouchard to obtain additional information about Monterey.

At last Bouchard was ready to attack Alta California. An unlikely collection of men of different races and languages, most of whom had no idea what the independence movement was all about, but all of whom were bound by a burning desire for adventure and money, Bouchard's crew approached Monterey.[3] What awaited them was the wide and beautiful bay of Monterey, with its barking sea lions, its seals, sea otters, pines, and cypresses—described by the exuberant Sebastián Vizcaíno a century and a half earlier in such fantastic terms that later explorers had difficulty finding it. Without its protective fog, the settlement lay open to their eager eyes just as their own sails became visible to the nervous lookout at Point Pinos.

Bouchard was about to face a major challenge. Alta California's social structure was very different from that of most of Spanish America. Here, the missions and presidios, deeply loyal to the crown, totally dominated the life of the province. There were no large ranchers or merchants itching to become independent. Of all the Spanish possessions in America, Alta California (along with Peru and Cuba) was the most loyal to the crown. Bouchard's only hope for success was to incite a popular uprising—to get the poor *mestizos* and Indians on his side. But the Indians had no reason to want to switch white masters, and the poor *mestizos* were insignificant as a force.

Bouchard had a decisive military advantage over the defenders of Monterey. His contingent, in fact, was almost as large as the entire armed forces of Alta California. *La Argentina*, later called by the Californians the fragata negra (black frigate), had 260 men and thirty-four 8- and 12-caliber guns. The *Santa Rosa* had 100 men and eighteen 12- and 18-caliber guns.[4]

The Plan That Failed

Privateers preferred to raid merchant ships. Merchant ships could not hide their riches. Mainlanders, on the other hand, if they were forewarned, had ample time to hide their valuables. Therefore, Bouchard did not want the defenders of Monterey to suspect that he was an enemy.

Bouchard's plan was to have the *Santa Rosa* enter the port flying the United States flag.[5] Corney would disembark to observe the defenses, including the number of troops. At night, Bouchard would come as close as possible with *La Argentina*, and the crews of the two ships would land and take the place by surprise.[6] What neither Bouchard nor Corney suspected was that more than a month before their arrival, the governor of Alta California had learned of their coming. When the two vessels approached Monterey, the governor was ready. The element of surprise was gone.

On November 20, the two vessels were spotted by the lookout at Point Pinos. The governor immediately ordered all the presidio soldiers and residents from the surrounding fifteen miles to gather at the gun battery.[7] He counted forty men ready to fight. Twenty-five were soldiers from the presidio. Mounted on horseback and dressed in leather jackets, leather pants, and wide-brimmed sombreros, they were the *soldados de cuera* (leather soldiers.) They were joined by four artillerymen and eleven militiamen. After exhorting them all to do their duty, the governor placed them under the command of officers Manuel Gómez and José Estrada.[8]

The small army was about to fight the largest battle in the history of Spanish Alta California. Poorly paid or not paid at all, almost forgotten in this remote outpost, they were about to defend the honor of their flag, the red and yellow colors of the kingdom of Spain. The foe, two menacing ships with overwhelming superiority in guns and men, were now in sight of the panicked residents of Monterey. Against such overwhelming odds, Governor Solá held one important card: he knew that they were coming and who they were. No matter what flags they displayed, what languages they spoke, he knew that they were insurgents from a rebellious faraway land coming to seize his province.

By late afternoon, Bouchard's frigate was five miles off the coast of Monterey. The wind died, and the privateers were forced to tow the vessel with their rowboats. By eleven at night they reached waters fifteen fathoms deep and anchored two miles from shore, "unable to come closer because of the calm wind and the current that was pulling away."[9]

By midnight Corney anchored the smaller *Santa Rosa* at less than a quarter of a mile from the fort.[10] The Spaniards shouted questions through the speaking trumpet, asking about the identity of the vessel and inviting them to send a boat ashore with the ship's papers. To hide their identity, Corney's men answered in English—"which nobody could understand"—but finally the Spaniards understood that the night was dark, and therefore the papers would be delivered in the morning. Unbeknownst to the Spaniards, feverish activity now started on both ships.

Keen to pursue a night attack, Bouchard sent his boats loaded with sailors to the *Santa Rosa*, ordering William Sheppard to land immediately with 200 men and take the fort by surprise.[11] Inexplicably, the order was not carried out, and the night went by without any action. One speculation is that

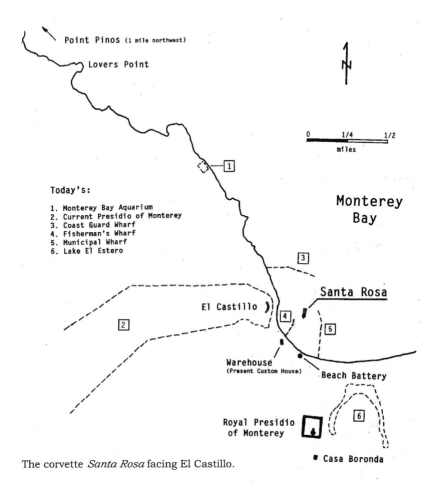

Point Pinos (1 mile northwest)

Lovers Point

N

0   1/4   1/2
miles

Monterey
Bay

Today's:

1. Monterey Bay Aquarium
2. Current Presidio of Monterey
3. Coast Guard Wharf
4. Fisherman's Wharf
5. Municipal Wharf
6. Lake El Estero

1

3

Santa Rosa

El Castillo

4

2

5

Warehouse
(Present Custom House)

Beach Battery

Royal Presidio
of Monterey

6

Casa Boronda

The corvette *Santa Rosa* facing El Castillo.

Sheppard was persuaded by his troops to wait until the next day because the soldiers were exhausted from pulling the frigate with the rowboats.[12] Bouchard was not happy. "Had this order been executed," he later said, "the fort would have fallen without a rifle shot."

For unknown reasons, the *Santa Rosa* remained anchored within the reach of the guns of Monterey. This was in spite of the fact that Corney knew the details about the Monterey's batteries from his visit three years ago.[13]

Before dawn, Corney noticed that the fort battery was already fully manned, and that the Spaniards "seemed quite busy." Obviously this was not the behavior of people who were just expecting a rowboat carrying the ship's papers. Something had happened—the Spaniards knew who they were. Corney decided not to wait for the Spanish guns to open fire but to take the initiative himself.[14]

At dawn, the *Santa Rosa*, revealing her identity, raised the flag of the Provincias Unidas and started firing at El Castillo.[15] The fort returned fire with its eight-gun battery, which was joined by a second battery installed on the beach, approximately 600 yards south of El Castillo.[16] Second Lieutenant Manuel Gómez was commanding both batteries from El Castillo, while Corporal José de Jesús Vallejo was in charge of the beach battery.[17]

The Monterey guns proved surprisingly accurate, and the *Santa Rosa* was hit repeatedly. Bouchard watched in horror as "after seven rounds of fire I saw with disgust our flag lowered and people escaping in boats toward my ship, four or five per boat."[18]

At this point, probably seeing that the *Santa Rosa* was beaten, Gómez ordered both batteries to cease-fire. The reason for *Santa Rosa*'s difficulties, wrote Corney, was that El Castillo's battery was so much higher than *Santa Rosa*'s "that our shot had no visible effect."[19] On the other hand, Solá praised the El Castillo battery crew for remaining in their places "with remarkable calm in spite of the many cannonballs falling on it." Not surprisingly, Corney, in his memoirs, does not mention the outcome of the gun battle or the surrender of the *Santa Rosa*.

The batteries of Monterey had won the battle. This was the only time in the history of California that a shore battery engaged in a gun battle with enemy ships.

While Corney in his writings avoided discussing the gun battle, local stories highlight it and add color to it. These stories include accounts such as that Bouchard had visited Monterey before his raid; he had sent an agent to spy; Manuel Gómez was a traitor who had sent Bouchard the plans of the Monterey defenses; the Vallejo's beach battery sunk one of the boats from the *Santa Rosa*, injuring or killing 30 men. But these events are unverified.[20]

When the *Santa Rosa* lowered her flag, Solá ordered that her commander be sent ashore. The answer from the corvette was that the commander had fled in one of the boats to the distant "fragata negra." Solá then sent word that "whoever was now commanding [the Santa Rosa] should come ashore, otherwise the firing would continue." No one was sent, and the firing resumed. This worked and the second in command, an American called Joseph Chapman, accompanied by a sailor from Buenos Aires and another from Guinea, went ashore. They did not provide enough information to satisfy Solá—"only lies and frivolous excuses"—so Solá ordered them imprisoned.[21]

The *Santa Rosa* had suffered five dead and a number of wounded. The Spaniards suffered no casualties—a miracle, Solá remarked, since the fight had lasted two hours.[22] For the rest of the day the corvette just sat there, undisturbed. In his report to the viceroy, the governor, always ready to complain about the lack of resources, pointed out that he had not sunk the ship because he had not had enough cannons, ammunition, and artillerymen, and that she had not been boarded because he had not had enough men and boats.[23] Bouchard agreed; he writes that it was fortunate that the Spaniards did not have boats to come to the corvette and take prisoners.

Why did the *Santa Rosa* engage in a disastrous gun battle with the batteries of Monterey? The participants do not say, so we can only guess. Ships in those times typically engaged in battle with other ships, facing each other and exchanging fire. Battles with shore batteries were avoided because the constant rolling of the ship made it difficult to aim the guns accurately. This gave the shore guns an advantage—especially if the target ship was anchored. Bouchard knew all this; thus the plan for a surprise night landing.

After Sheppard postponed the night landing, Corney could have moved away from shore. Why did he not do so? Had he anchored in shallow waters during high tide and become stuck at low tide? A calculation of the tides for that day shows just the opposite: the *Santa Rosa* anchored in low tide and the high tide occurred the next morning, just before the gun battle.[24] The most likely reason why Corney, a merchant sailor, engaged in battle with the shore guns is that, based on his previous visit to Monterey, he simply underestimated their guns and their artillerymen. He did not believe that they could hit him. He believed that all he needed to do was to fire a few salvos with his superior gun power, and the shore defenders would give up. It turned out that he was badly mistaken. Did Bouchard, anchored in the darkness two miles away, know that Sheppard was not planning to disembark at night? Most likely he did not; otherwise he would have ordered the *Santa Rosa* to withdraw.

At any rate, the "fragata negra" remained anchored far from shore for the entire day. According to Bouchard, she could not come closer. According to Solá, she stopped out of range of the shore guns. The *Santa Rosa* was powerless, and Bouchard, realizing that he needed to gain time, sent an emissary ashore. The emissary delivered an ultimatum requesting the surrender of the entire province—a somewhat surprising request coming from a position of weakness, but certainly effective in gaining time. To which, the governor wrote:

> I replied that the governor of this province looked with due contempt on everything said in that note; that the great monarch whom I was serving had entrusted to my authority the preservation of the province to remain under his domain; that as he was threatening with the use of his force, I would with mine make him know the honor and firmness with which I was ready to repel him; that as long as there remained a man alive in this province he would not succeed in his intent because all the inhabitants were loyal and loving servants of the king; and that they would spill their last drop of blood in his service.[25]

José María Piriz, the commander of Bouchard's marines, writes that Solá also asked for money to return the corvette. This contributed, Piriz said, to Bouchard's anger and his decision to land at all cost.[26]

At the end of the first day, things looked good for the Spaniards. One of the rebel ships had capitulated after suffering severe losses, and three prisoners had been taken. Bouchard's demand for surrender had been rejected, and the larger ship lay at a distance, where she could not inflict any damage.

According to Solá, his troops remained vigilant all night under a heavy rain. In contrast, Bouchard wrote, the enemy was celebrating at the fort with a dancing party. If there was a celebration, it was premature.

The Plan That Worked

During that night, Bouchard, taking advantage of what he said was a noisy party, sent his boats to the *Santa Rosa* to rescue anyone left there. All the able men were retrieved to *La Argentina*. Only the wounded were left behind, to avoid warning the enemy by their cries if they were moved. Now Bouchard himself was ready for action.

The next morning, November 22, 200 men, including 13 officers (but without Sheppard),[27] embarked in nine boats with Bouchard as their leader. One hundred thirty were armed with muskets and the rest with spears. Four of the boats carried one small cannon each.[28]

The boats landed around eight o'clock in the vicinity of what is today's Lovers Point.[29] Solá, realizing that they were about to attack the fort, sent Ensign José Estrada with his twenty-five soldiers to observe them. Estrada sent back reports at frequent intervals and Solá became very worried. "I learned that they had disembarked with 400 men and four cannons," he wrote to the viceroy, "seeing at the same time the two enemy vessels dueling with our battery, what could I do, Your Excellency, in such a situation?"[30] The governor ordered Estrada to retreat to the fort and, if necessary, to spike all the guns, blow up the remaining gunpowder, and retreat to the presidio.

Bouchard's small army advanced through gentle hills cov-

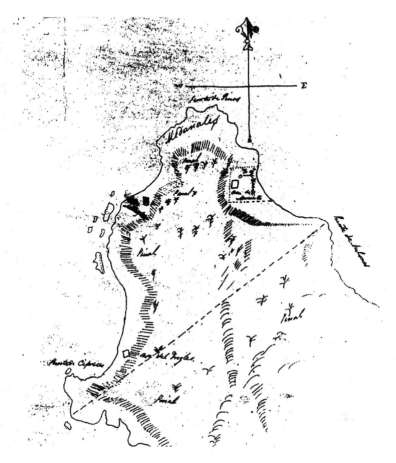

Bouchard's landing place at Monterey. Mexican-period map (Land Case 169 SD) showing Casa de Armenta opposite today's Lovers Point (the landing place). Courtesy of The Bancroft Library, University of California, Berkeley.

ered by wet pine trees and sagebrush, probably along what is now Hawthorne Street, passing near the site of Cannery Row and the Monterey Bay Aquarium.[31] They met no resistance and by ten in the morning had occupied El Castillo.[32] The Hawaiians with their spears led the charge, and it was an Hawaiian who first hauled down the colors of Spain. The Spaniards mounted their horses and fled.[33]

The insurgents now turned their guns on the presidio, where the Spaniards were taking a stand. After firing a few rounds, Bouchard sent Corney to seize the place. The participants differ as to what happened next. Corney wrote that, "as we approached the town, the Spaniards again fled, after discharging their field-pieces, and we entered without opposition."[34] Solá reported that his men offered "some resistance."[35] Piriz, on the other hand, wrote that "they offered quite some resistance for which reason we took the pueblo by blood and fire."[36] This statement is somewhat suspect, since Solá reported to his viceroy that his forces sustained no casualties from the raid.

The Spaniards had lost the battle for Monterey. Solá and his troops retreated to the Rancho del Rey, taking with them one small cannon, two boxes of gunpowder, 6,000 musket cartridges, and the provincial archives. Prior to this, civilians had been sent away, some as far as Mission Soledad some forty miles distant. The exodus was a traumatic experience for the fleeing families, as Dorotea Valdéz, an eyewitness, recounted: "Early in the morning of that fatal day Governor Solá ordered the women, old men and children to be driven to the woods. I assure you that they drove us away in a hurry for the greater part of us went away almost naked and among the whole lot there were but two persons that wore shoes . . . after remaining two days in the Rancho del Rey we returned."[37]

Whatever the form of the retreat, by the time the insurgents arrived there were no prisoners to be taken or people to talk to. One exception was a drunken settler named Molina, who either stayed behind or wandered into town later. Bancroft writes, "it was never clearly known whether he had deserted to the insurgents, had really been taken prisoner, or had gone on board the ship too drunk to know his mind." This was the only person Bouchard took prisoner in Alta California.

With the flag of the Provincias Unidas now flying at Monterey, the victors started "searching the houses for money, and breaking and ruining every thing" according to Peter Corney. Because the raid had not been a surprise, it is doubtful that they found any money or valuables. The presidio, on the other hand was "well stocked with provisions and goods of every description, which we commenced sending on board the *Argentina*." He adds: "The Sandwich Islanders [the Hawaiians], who were quite naked when they landed, were soon dressed in the Spanish fashion."

Could the appearance of the attackers have contributed to their fame as pirates? They certainly looked different from the sailors on the few ships that had stopped at Monterey. It is possible that the appearance and actions of the rough-looking privateers convinced the Californians that they were just plain pirates.

"After doing the wicked things the rebels do by custom," the governor wrote, "like relieving their rage by shooting the animals they found, because they could not shoot people, they stole whatever they found useful in the midst of the poverty in which these people live." Solá estimated that 2,000 pesos were lost in supplies like ham, butter, and blankets, "and some other things of little value belonging to our soldiers. I lost all my furniture and other things that I need very much."[38]

Meanwhile, the governor's forces at the Rancho del Rey received reinforcements from San Francisco and San José. However, they did not attack, content to observe the enemy and "to hinder the pirates, foes of the human race, from going inland,

. . . [they] have not dared to cross over to San Carlos [Carmel Mission]" said Solá, taking some credit for this outcome. Bouchard, however, was not keen on pillaging churches. They remained untouched at every one of his stops in California. "He was no worse than the Spaniards," wrote José de Jesús Vallejo, the artilleryman at the beach battery, in his memoirs half a century later.

On the third day, Corney reported that "a party of horsemen came in sight, to whom the Commodore sent a flag of truce, requiring the governor to give up our people and save the town. Three days were granted to consider this proposal, and on the third day, not receiving an answer, he ordered the town to be fired."

All the houses on the northern side of the presidio and three houses on the southern side were burned, as well as the building housing the artillerymen at El Castillo. Since all of the presidio houses were built of adobe, what burned were the roof beams. The privateers did not, however, damage the presidio church, nor did they touch the Mission at Carmel.[39] According to Bouchard, he destroyed everything belonging to the king, saving only the churches and the houses of the Americans (meaning probably "non-Spaniards"), and taking two guns for the *Santa Rosa*.[40] One of the eyewitnesses later said, "with the assistance of carpenters, blacksmiths and many neophytes in less than four months our city looked as smart as before."[41]

In her duel with the batteries, the *Santa Rosa* had taken about ten hits, most of which went clear through the ship, from one side to the other. Bouchard assigned all his carpenters to make repairs. This is probably the reason why the rebels remained at Monterey until about November 27,[42] when they left for Rancho del Refugio, 200 miles to the south.[43]

Solá now had to worry about the rest of the province. Where would Bouchard strike next? The nearby settlement of Santa Cruz was certainly a candidate.

The Looting at Santa Cruz

Although the military forces of the province were on a war footing, not everyone was eager to fight. The raid created a major controversy at the Mission of Santa Cruz.

Even before Bouchard's arrival, Padre Ramón Olbés of the Santa Cruz Mission accused the settlers of the pueblo of Branciforte of intending to join the rebels in a raid on the mission.[44] The town's *mestizos* were not held in high regard by the local Spaniards, some of them being petty criminals from Mexico. Also, they were less loyal to Spain than the missionaries or the presidio officers and were, therefore, suspected of being potential rebels.

Anticipating that the insurgents might come to Santa Cruz, Solá ordered Padre Olbés to leave with his neophytes for the Mission of Santa Clara. After he left, Solá had second thoughts. Not wanting to leave anything behind for the insurgents, he ordered the leader of Branciforte, Joaquin Buelna, to remove everything of value from the mission. Buelna and his helpers forced the mission doors open and set to work. At this point, some members of Padre Olbés' party, who had also had second thoughts, returned to save some of the mission goods. Upon being informed of the governor's orders, they enthusiastically joined in the efforts of Buelna and his people. In their haste, Bancroft tells us:

> One or two casks of wine and aguardiente that could
> not be carried away it was deemed best to spill, not
> improbably in the throats of those present. After this
> the work went bravely on, but naturally the goods
> were not "saved" with the systematic care that would
> have been desired by the friars . . . and it is by no
> means unlikely that in the confusion a few trifles
> were appropriated by both settlers and Indians.[45]

But Bouchard never got to Santa Cruz, and when he saw
the damage, Padre Olbés was furious. "The establishment must
be abandoned," Olbés declared, for he "would not go back to
submit longer to the inhuman outrages of the people of
Branciforte."[46] The incident forced Solá to start an investigation that lasted several months. Joaquin Buelna, a respected
leader, was cleared of all charges.

The Raid on Refugio

On December 4, the privateers landed at the Ortega's Rancho
del Refugio, some twenty-three miles north of Santa Barbara.[47]
The Ortegas were believed to be smugglers who kept large
amounts of money and valuables at the rancho.[48] Since the
only local contact for the privateers had been Molina, it is likely
that Bouchard got this information from him. However, it is
also possible that Corney had obtained it on his previous visit
to Monterey. Bouchard said that the reason he went to the
Rancho del Refugio was because it was the ranch of a Spaniard
who, "according to the information I had, was one who had
tormented Mexican patriots."

Sixty men disembarked while the inhabitants of the ranch fled. The next morning, the place was plundered while the Spaniards observed from a distance. One of Bouchard's officers and two seamen strayed a short distance from the ranch, and according to Corney, "a party of horsemen rushed on them, threw the lassos over their heads and dragged them up a neighboring hill, before we could render them any assistance." The capture of the three men enraged Bouchard, who ordered the village burned. That night, Bouchard's men tried to surprise the Spaniards who had retreated but were still in the vicinity, and take some prisoners of his own, but without success. As by now the entire province had been warned of the expected invasion, it is unlikely that Bouchard found any money or valuables at Rancho del Refugio either.

Guessing that the three men the Spaniards had captured had been taken to the nearest presidio, Bouchard headed for Santa Barbara. Sailing two miles from shore he was being followed by "a great number of Spanish troops riding along the beach at whom we fired several shots."[49] The rebel attack had put the entire province of Alta California in a frantic defensive mood. The scant troops were being shifted among the presidios and Bouchard's various landing places. Santa Barbara, for example, had sent help north upon hearing of the Monterey landing, only to have its men sent back south as soon as Bouchard's ships left. Solá, in his report to the viceroy, praised the Spanish troops' efforts to keep up with the enemy over long distances. Somewhat self-servingly, he added that as soon as his own troops reached sufficient numbers, even if not half the enemy numbers, but eager to attack—the insurgents would pack up and leave.[50]

One group that was eager to fight was, as Bancroft calls them, the "fighting friars." The missionaries were powerful and unquestioningly loyal to Spain. They armed some neophytes and got ready for action. One of the padres affirmed that they would perform deeds "that should be recorded in characters of gold."[51] Padre Martínez from San Luis Obispo took thirty-five neophytes to the scene of action at Rancho del Refugio. There they joined a contingent of thirty men that had come from Santa Barbara. From a distance, they watched the rebel raid. The excitement produced some exaggerations. One witness, for example, said that he saw 500 rebels in a single house.

Solá, in his report of the invasion, does not mention the contributions of the Spanish padres, thus the later praises from the viceroy did not include them. The friars complained to the governor, who sent a supplementary report setting the record straight, and Viceroy Juan Ruiz de Apodaca formally thanked the padres in the name of the king.

The Stop at Santa Barbara

In the evening of December 8, 1818, Bouchard's small fleet arrived at Santa Barbara.[52] From a distance of one mile, the town seemed deserted. If Bouchard had been unable to surprise the Spaniards during his first stop at Monterey, he knew that he had even less chances of surprising them in Santa Barbara. He wrote that he went to Santa Barbara because he assumed that that was where the three prisoners from Refugio had been taken and he wanted to get them back. "We fired a gun," Corney wrote, "and hoisted the colors with a flag of truce, and sent a boat on shore to say if they would give up our men we would spare the town; to which the governor agreed, and accordingly, on the 10th we got our companions on board, weighed the anchor and made sail to the southward."[53] The "governor" was the commander of the Presidio of Santa Barbara, Don José de la Guerra y Noriega.

The three prisoners were exchanged for the drunken Molina, seized at Monterey. Bouchard also promised that he would not stop at any other points in Alta California.[54] Solá later sentenced the unfortunate Molina, who was something of a celebrity by now, to 100 lashes, followed by six years in the chain gang. The poor man—who had done nothing worse than to be in the wrong place at the wrong time—was eventually hired as a servant at de la Guerra's household, where he remained until the end of his days.[55]

Solá was critical of de la Guerra because he had exchanged three prisoners for one, and because he had failed to take action against the rebels. This last was a surprising criticism, since Solá himself had not taken offensive action at Monterey, even though his forces were superior to de la Guerra's forces at Santa Barbara.[56] Furthermore, the rebels had ravaged Monterey, while no damage had been done at Santa Barbara. De la Guerra's other critics included a padre who—somewhat unexpectedly for a friar—suggested that the women of Santa Barbara should not have been sent away upon Bouchard's approach, for had they remained, "the insurgents yielding to their charms might have fallen an easy prey to the military force."[57]

The Raid on San Juan Capistrano

On December 16, 1818, the two vessels reached San Juan

Capistrano, about 120 miles south of Santa Barbara.[58] Although, according to de la Guerra, the rebels had given their word not to stop on the Alta California coast anymore, they had obviously changed their minds. Peter Corney described what happened next:

> We run into a snug bay . . . where we anchored under the flag of truce. The bay is well sheltered, with a most beautiful town and mission, about two leagues from the beach. The Commodore sent his boat on shore, to say if they would give us an immediate supply of provisions we would spare their town; to which they replied, that we might land if we pleased, and they would give us an immediate supply of powder and shot. The Commodore was very much incensed at this answer, and assembled all officers, to know what was best to be done, as the town was too far from the beach to derive any benefit from it. It was, therefore, agreed to land, and give it up to be pillaged and sacked. Next morning, before daylight, the Commodore ordered me to land and bring him a sample of the powder and shot, which I accordingly did, with a party of 140 men, well armed, with two field pieces.[59] On our landing a party of horsemen came down and fired a few shots at us, and ran towards the town. They made no stand, and we soon occupied the place. After breakfast the people commenced plundering; we found the town well stocked with every thing but money and destroyed much wine and spirits, and all the public property; set fire to

the king's stores, barracks, and governor's house, and about two o'clock we marched back, though not in the order we went, many of the men being intoxicated, and some were so much so, that we had to lash them on the field pieces and drag them to the beach, where, about six o'clock, we arrived with the loss of six men. Next morning we punished about twenty men for getting drunk.[60]

Four men—three Americans (non-Spaniards) and one Englishman—deserted the rebels at San Juan Capistrano, claiming that they had been forced to come with Bouchard's party. [61] Bouchard, thinking that the four men had been ambushed, threatened to burn "the church and the houses of the civilians" unless they were returned but gave up when the written reply convinced him that they were, in fact, deserters.[62]

Before the raid, Solá had sent 30 soldiers from San Diego to Capistrano, and the day after the raid 84 more men arrived from Santa Barbara.[63] Don José de la Guerra y Noriega, who had arrived with the contingent from Santa Barbara, challenged the rebels to come ashore again, but they ignored him and sailed away.

Thus ended Bouchard's raid on Alta California.

Farewell to California

In defending Alta California against the rebels, Solá had shown wisdom and prudence—if not heroism. Accounts, written more than half a century later, tell of heroic events, but they are unsubstantiated. The historian Bancroft, for example, cites the story told by Mariano G. Vallejo, where the Spaniards surprised

80 of Bouchard's men climbing the hills by Rancho del Refugio, and rolled stones down upon them killing five and wounding two.[64] One indication that these battles probably did not happen is that Solá, in his report to the viceroy, does not mention any of them—although he eagerly highlights any small fact that might make the defenders look brave.[65] On the other hand, his strategy of retreating from the rebels, taking all of the valuables and civilians with him, proved sound. Although the province suffered material damage, no one was killed and the valuables were saved. Bouchard did not come in contact with the population, and the province remained loyal to Spain. The impression the privateers left in California was that they were a group of tough looking men who behaved violently—just like, well, pirates.

As a result of the raid, Solá was promoted to colonel, Manuel Gómez and José Estrada were promoted to lieutenants, and Viceroy Apodaca sent arms and additional 200 soldiers to Alta California.[66]

These men proved more of a burden than a relief to California, for many of them belonged to the "criminal and vagabond classes," according to Bancroft. Solá complained bitterly about the quality of men and arms he was sent. He received a severe reprimand from the viceroy, who was astounded by Solá's impudence and ingratitude—"if the two hundred men I have sent are of no use to you, send them back." Selected neophytes were organized by some missions into fighting units, some bearing bows, others machetes or lances. These Indians promised to shed their last drop of blood for their king; their arms were, however, locked up, and the head of Alta California missions, Padre Payeras, doubted the Indian's conduct in battle.[67]

Another effect of Bouchard's raid was that the Anglo-Saxon population of Alta California increased from three to five persons. One of the two newcomers was Joseph Chapman, one of Bouchard's officers taken prisoners at Monterey; the other was the Scottish drummer John Rose, who deserted from the insurgents at San Juan Capistrano. To be accepted as residents of Alta California, both men eventually had to convert to Catholicism. Joseph Chapman, purportedly convinced of "how mistaken he had been when he lived within the sect of the Anabaptists, resolved to forsake it and embrace that most holy one." Accordingly, he "had the glory of receiving baptism from that holy man Padre Señán."[68] John Rose may have been a more difficult case for he was "so far astray that it was deemed unsafe to expose the Indians of San Diego to his influence."[69]

Bouchard had inflicted damage on the king's property and had heightened Alta California's awareness of the insurgency against Spain. His incursion on Alta California served as a mighty warning to the easygoing province of things to come. After he left Alta California, the panicked viceroy was forced to divert troops and arms to the forgotten province and away from the main theater of revolutionary activities in Mexico. On the downside, Bouchard had lost three men as prisoners; four men had deserted; five had died and an indeterminate number were wounded. The corvette had also suffered considerable damage. In addition, he had not gotten in touch with the people of Alta California and thus could not assess their feelings about the insurgency against Spain.[70] The province remained a remote spectator to the revolution with no impact on either side of the Spanish-American wars of independence.

Had Alta California embraced Bouchard, could he have

changed the course of history? This is highly unlikely. Although joining the revolt against Spain might have delayed or even eliminated Mexican rule, the forces of Manifest Destiny would ultimately have prevailed, and Alta California would still have become part of the United States.

Bouchard must have been deeply disappointed not to find more riches in Alta California. He had a large crew, all waiting for the end of the voyage and their share of the prizes. But there were no prizes. By now it was time to head for home and he urgently wanted to make some profit from this long and painful voyage. Up to this point, the determined captain had been in his element. His bravery and determination had overcome all obstacles. The events that were to follow, however, forced Bouchard into a corner from which there was no escape.

IV. *Return and Exile*

Heading Home

From San Juan Capistrano, Bouchard and Corney sailed south along an increasingly arid coast. On December 24, 1818, the two ships stopped at Cedros Island off Baja California. They made repairs, hunted deer, and "[killed] the sea lion and elephant for the sake of their hearts and tongues, which we found very good." They also had parties with ambitious otter-hunting Russians who had been left there by an American vessel. The otherwise restful stay was marred by the desertion of five former mutineers from the *Santa Rosa* who had joined Bouchard in Hawaii. "Captain Bouchard swore if he caught them he would immediately execute them,"[1] Corney writes. However, they got away.

On January 18 the ships put to sea again, arriving at the islands of Tres Marías (off the coast of Nayarit, Mexico). Here Bouchard wrote his first trip report of the voyage, which he sent to Buenos Aires via an English ship. His frustration shows in the report. "I have run from one extreme to the other," he writes, "but did not have the luck of finding a single ship with the Spanish flag since my departure from Buenos Aires on June 27, 1817, up to my arrival at the islands of Tres Marías on the

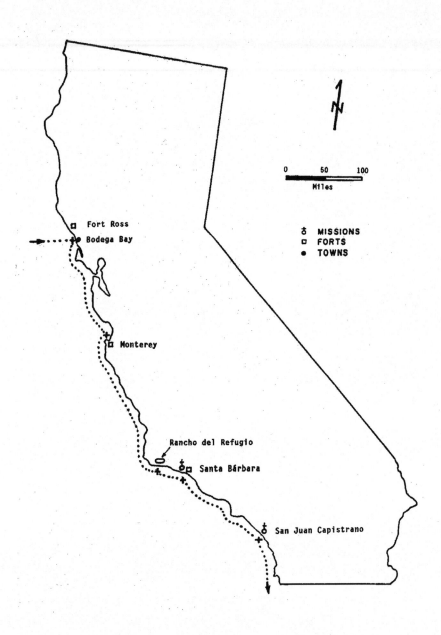

Bouchard's stops in Alta California.

coast of Baja California." The report, which details Bouchard's adventures, undoubtedly caused a sensation in Buenos Aires. The proud owner of *La Argentina*, Anastasio Echevarría, had the report published, making Bouchard a popular hero in his adopted country.

Continuing south down the coast of Mexico, Bouchard looked for Spanish vessels off San Blas and Acapulco. Finally, his perseverance paid off. At Realejo, Nicaragua, the rebels seized four vessels. Bouchard designated two of them, the *María Sophie* and the *Neptuno*, as privateers and incorporated them into his growing fleet. The other two vessels, the *Laurentana* and the *San Antonio*, were destroyed. The reason was, Piriz wrote, that their owners offered only 10,000 pesos to let the two ships go, but "since our objective was not just money but the weakening of their naval forces, we set them afire in front of their own eyes after taking their guns and prisoners."[2]

Bouchard was now commanding a squadron of four vessels. The next resupply point was to be Valparaíso, Chile, an ally of the Provincias Unidas del Río de la Plata. Chile was the country that his former commander, José de San Martín, had helped liberate shortly before Bouchard left on his long voyage. Finally, Bouchard would be among friends.

The *Santa Rosa* and the *María Sophie*, with Corney in command, were the first to arrive at Valparaíso—on July 9, 1819, exactly two years after Bouchard's departure from Buenos Aires.[3] Three days later, the *Neptuno* arrived and then *La Argentina* under Bouchard's command.[4] The noted Chilean historian Diego Barros Arana reported what happened next, and the following account is based largely on his description.[5]

Disaster at Valparaíso

During the night of July 9, a boat from the Corney contingent carefully approached the port. Most likely this was to make sure that the port was in friendly hands. After a short inspection, the boat tried to leave, but its crew was arrested. Vice Admiral Cochrane,[6] a Scotsman at the service of Chile, having been informed of the arrest, sent out a brigantine to look for the vessel where these men came from. She returned with two vessels flying the Argentine flag but without valid privateering papers. Furthermore, one of them, the *María Sophie* turned out to be a Danish vessel, illegally seized, whose captain and crew were being held prisoners under brutal conditions.

From the freed prisoners, the Chileans learned that these Argentine privateers had plundered an English vessel off the Sunda Strait, Indonesia. The word spread, and the commander of the British naval forces in the Pacific, Captain Shirref, immediately demanded a full investigation.

Vice Admiral Cochrane concluded that the crews in control of the two captured ships were pirates. He decided that energetic measures, such as a trial and seizure of the ships for use by the state, were needed to put the Chilean navy in a respectable light in the eyes of the Europeans.

When Bouchard arrived, he was indignant. He expected, if not a hero's welcome, at least a friendly reception. After all, during his voyage around the world he had captured twenty-six ships and engaged in ten naval battles and three land battles. On the afternoon of his arrival, a captain of the Chilean navy and a captain of the British navy came on board *La Argentina* to register the vessel and to get information about the alleged acts of piracy. Bouchard, offended by the treatment he was receiving, ordered his men to threaten the visitors with their bayonets. Cochrane sent his troops to seize the frigate, and Bouchard was thrown into prison.

The government of Chile found itself in an embarrassing position. Bouchard's men had threatened a Chilean official. In addition, Captain Shirref, who was representing Great Britain and who had powerful vessels at his command, wanted action to be taken, as did an influential local Dane who represented the captain of the *María Sophie*. Bouchard was put on trial in front of a prize court.

Unfortunately for Bouchard, General San Martín, his former commander, was not in Valparaíso during his arrest and subsequent trial. A man of unquestionable influence in Chile, San Martín lay ill in the Provincias Unidas, across the Andes some 300 miles away. Would San Martín have helped Bouchard by telling the court how Bouchard had served the Provincias Unidas? We will never know.

By now most of Bouchard's squadron crew had joined the Chilean fleet. Peter Corney also wanted out: "I now applied to Captain Bouchard for my pay and prize-money, and told him I was heartily sick of the service of the Independents, and that I intended to go to England in the first vessel that sailed for that country . . . he replied that he could not pay me, unless I continued in the service and took the ship to Buenos Ayres: which I declined doing."[7]

What Is a Pirate?

According to the accusers, Bouchard was a pirate—a grave accusation punishable by death—because he had taken goods from several non-Spanish ships. In addition, he had captured the *María Sophie*, a Danish vessel, and turned her into an armed privateer at a time when he himself was not a valid privateer, and without first having her condemned as a valid prize.[8] Bouchard defended himself by claiming that his letter of marque had expired because he had learned of the *Santa Rosa* mutiny while he was in the Sunda Strait and had gone on a state mission to Hawaii to recapture the *Santa Rosa* from the pirates. Therefore, he argued, he should be given credit for the time it had taken him to complete this mission.[9] This argument stretched the truth somewhat. Before he ever reached Valparaíso, Bouchard had written in his trip report that he had learned about the *Santa Rosa* mutiny only after he arrived in Hawaii. However, the man had to defend himself, and calling the recapture of *Santa Rosa* a state mission seemed reasonable, regardless of when he had learned about the mutiny.

Then, there was the question whether the *María Sophie* was at the service of Spain when he had captured her. Since Spain, Bouchard argued, allowed only Spanish (or Spanish-authorized) vessels to do business in its colonies, the *María Sophie* must have been Spanish. Otherwise "the captain that entered Realejo without Spanish papers would have been a madman."[10]

On December 7, 1819, the prize court delivered its ruling. Bouchard was to be set free, and all seized ships were to be returned to him. As for the resistance he had shown to the Chilean authorities when he arrived in Valparaíso, the court asked the Provincias Unidas to provide satisfaction to the government of Chile. The ruling did not mention the alleged plundering of an English vessel in the Sunda Strait. The implication was that the case should be continued before the courts of Buenos Aires.[11]

Some Argentine historians believe that Cochrane's stated reason for seizing Bouchard's ships was not his real reason. At the time, Cochrane was getting ready a squadron that he and San Martín were to use to attack the Spaniards in Peru. Therefore, Cochrane's real reason for seizing the ships, says one, was that he needed money to pay for his squadron, and perhaps even for his own personal benefit.[12] Another historian surmises that Cochrane seized Bouchard's ships because he disliked the Argentine hero San Martín.[13]

The Years in Peru[14]

Painfully aware of the importance of holding valid letters of marque, Bouchard now asked Echevarría for a new letter for each of the four ships. The letters were issued in January 1820. They were valid for eight months—long enough to get the ships back to Buenos Aires. Bouchard sent the *María Sophie* and the *Neptuno* to the Provincias Unidas, allowing Echevarría to recover some of his investment. Echevarría sold the *María Sophie* for 4,315 pesos, but this was not even close to the partnership's investment in *La Argentina*, which was 82,000 pesos.[15] The *Santa Rosa* and *La Argentina*, in poor shape after the long and stressful voyage and stripped of much of their equipment during Bouchard's imprisonment, stayed with him in Chile.

Valparaíso was now buzzing with excitement and activity. San Martín, after his spectacular crossing of the Andes and liberation of Chile in 1817, had set his sights on Lima, Peru, the fortress of Spanish colonial power in South America. It was to be a seaborne invasion. Crews were being hired and ships of war and transports were being equipped. In spite of their poor conditions, the *Santa Rosa* and *La Argentina* were still good as transports, and for a fee of seven pesos per day per ton, the combined weight of 800 tons for both ships could produce a respectable revenue. Bouchard joined San Martín's expedition with the two vessels as transports.

On August 21, 1820, eight ships of war and thirty transports, the largest armada ever assembled in the Spanish-American wars of independence, left Valparaíso heading north for the coast of Peru. San Martín was the commander in chief of the combined Argentine-Chilean Expeditionary Force. Bouchard's nemesis, Lord Cochrane, was the commander of the fleet. Although San Martín and Cochrane disagreed on many aspects of the campaign, they succeeded and by mid 1821 San Martín was in Lima proclaiming Peru's independence. However, it would take three more years and the intervention of Simón Bolívar to end the Spanish rule.

Transporting troops was something new for the fierce and independent privateer. But Bouchard had not lost his flair for action. Although the governments and the people of the United States and Great Britain were sympathetic to the rebels during the Spanish-American wars of independence, their merchants traded with both sides. Often, they supplied both the royalists and the rebels with arms and provisions. Consequently, the insurgents looked at American and English ships with suspicion. In September 1821, Bouchard detained two English ships in the Peruvian port of Pisco, accusing them of lacking proper documents and of smuggling. A tribunal in Lima declared the two ships "good prizes." Bouchard evaluated the two prizes at

95,000 pesos, but it is not known whether he got any portion of the booty, for his new letters of marque had, again, expired.

At about the same time, in October 1821, the government of Buenos Aires decreed the end of its privateering program. It would not issue new letters of marque—unless events forced it to do so. Holders of current letters had to surrender them within eight months or risk being declared pirates. This was bad news for Bouchard, the privateer par excellence. Clearly, the war—his bread and butter—had shifted from the Provincias Unidas to Peru, making a return to Buenos Aires less and less appealing.

The End of a Friendship

Bouchard's increasing bickering with Buenos Aires about money added to these discouraging events. Upon his arrival in Peru, Bouchard wrote to his friend Echevarría that he was trying to put together the promised funds, upon which "I will return to Buenos Aires to give account of my expedition." Later he brooded that he had not yet received a penny in Peru. And how about the money that was owed him from the 1816 cruise with the *Halcón* in the South Pacific? Bouchard asked his friend.

The friendship between Bouchard and Echevarría slowly deteriorated, and by 1822 they had broken off relations completely. Echevarría continued to pressure Bouchard to account for what was due to him. The stridency of the allegations increased, as Echevarría accused Bouchard of keeping "portions of silver bars, claimed stolen when I have documents to the contrary; boxes of jewelry whose existence is denied but I have witnesses to affirm their existence; all the valuables in the vessels . . . worth many thousands." Then there was "Bouchard's assertion that the *Santa Rosa* was not part of the Expedition [the voyage around the world] because he bought her with his own money . . . even though he did not take a single peso when he left with *La Argentina*."[16]

For the owners of *La Argentina*, Bouchard's voyage had ended in total failure. In 1852, reflecting on past events, Echevarría wrote that of the 82,000 pesos invested in the frigate and the 109,000 pesos owed to him for services that Bouchard rendered on behalf of Peru, he did not get a penny.[17] Bouchard's enemies' warning upon his departure from Buenos Aires in 1817 may now have seemed prophetic to the unhappy Echevarría: Bouchard "stole the ship to use for his own benefit."

In 1822, after five years under the command of the fiery Frenchman, the proud frigate *La Argentina* had decayed to the point that she had to be dismantled into scrap wood. Unquestionably, this was a financial blow to Echevarría. However, to Bouchard it was an emotional blow as well. The adventures he had experienced while in command of the frigate, had represented the height of his career.

The corvette *Santa Rosa* continued transport services under Bouchard's command. But by 1823, both the *Santa Rosa* and her captain had come under scrutiny by the commander of the incipient Peruvian navy, Vice Admiral Martin J. Guise, a Britisher at the service of Peru. He noticed that Bouchard had no valid license, and that the service contract with the government was more advantageous to Bouchard than to the state. He recommended that the *Santa Rosa* be taken from Bouchard as a prize. Inexplicably, no action was taken, and Guise continued to give Bouchard ever more important assignments. No doubt his experience and bravery were valuable to Peru's incipient navy.

In February 1824, while the corvette *Santa Rosa* was anchored in the bay of Callao, a Spanish uprising took place, and the corvette, along with other ships, was captured by the enemy. The insurgents, with an eager Bouchard as volunteer, counterattacked but could not rescue two of the captured ships, so the rebels set them afire. In a report to Simón Bolívar, Bouchard was cited for bravery but at a high cost—one of the burned vessels was the *Santa Rosa.*

By now, Peru was Bouchard's home and he had no intention of returning to Buenos Aires. He had a "brilliant social position," wrote a member of the Peruvian navy.[18] However, his wife, Norberta Merlo de Bouchard, complained from Buenos Aires that he was not supporting his family although he was employed by the Peruvian navy.[19] Bouchard got to know his first daughter Carmen while living in Buenos Aires, but not his second daughter Fermina, born shortly after he left on his voyage around the world. Interestingly, the last ship Bouchard owned was called *Joven Fermina* (Young Fermina).

By 1826, the Spanish-American wars of independence were over. But expelling the Spaniards was one thing; becoming successful independent countries was quite another. The newly formed republics now sank into half a century of turmoil. A war erupted between Peru and Gran Colombia (today's Colombia, Venezuela, and Ecuador), whose president was the visionary Simón Bolívar. The Peruvians blockaded Guayaquil, where the commander of the Peruvian navy, Vice Admiral Guise, was killed in action in 1828. On January 19, 1829, Bouchard took his place—the most exalted position of his career.

Bouchard held this position until May 1829, when an accidental fire destroyed the frigate *Libertad*, the flagship of the Peruvian forces. Bouchard, her commander, was found responsible, and was removed from his position. This ended his career in the Peruvian navy; he retired with the rank of captain.[20]

Now in his fifties—an advanced age for those times—Bouchard concentrated on his retirement. As payment for due services, and in spite of protests on the part of Echevarría, who still was fighting for what was due him, the Peruvian government gave Bouchard two ranches in the province of Nazca, Peru.[21] Bouchard spent his last years as a gentleman farmer, growing grapes for the production of brandy.

His end came suddenly. Little is known about Bouchard's death beyond what is written on his death certificate dated January 6, 1837: "Navy Captain Hipólito Bouchard, of more than sixty years of age, was suddenly killed by his own slaves two nights ago at seven, for which reason he did not express his last will nor did he receive any sacraments."[22]

Did Bouchard mistreat his slaves? Or was he just a tired old man robbed and killed by greedy men? Like much of Bouchard's life, this remains a mystery. He was buried in the nearby church of San Francisco de Javier[23] and the government took over the farms.

Epilogue

Bouchard

In 1962, a century and a quarter after Bouchard's death, two men, armed with an electric lantern, candles, and an order by the president of Peru, descended into the crypt of the church of San Francisco de Javier. After examining two rows of fifty-two poorly marked and unmarked niches, they identified the remains of Capitán de Navío Hipólito Bouchard—"the remains of

Bouchard's resting place in the Panteón Naval of the Chacarita cemetery in Buenos Aires.

a white person, tall, therefore different from the inhabitants of this area."[24]

A few weeks later, on July 31, 1962, following a solemn ceremony, an Argentine cruiser, interestingly called *La Argentina*, took Bouchard's remains from Callao, Peru, to Buenos Aires, where Bouchard is considered a hero of the American wars of independence against Spain. He lies, side by side with other navy officers, in the Naval Mausoleum of the cemetery of Chacarita, Buenos Aires, the cemetery of the common people.

Bouchard's flair, adventures, and bravery have captured the public imagination in Argentina. Several schools and four ships were named after him, the latest a destroyer that took part in the Falklands war against Great Britain. A street and a small plaza in Buenos Aires, close to the waters of the Río de la Plata, carry his name. A medium-sized bust of the hero sits in the middle of the modest plaza, not far from an imposing monument to his former commander, General San Martín, who, mounted on a magnificent horse, dominates the beautiful Plaza San Martín.

On the other hand, the impression that Bouchard left in California was a negative one. Starting from the time of the raids, when a population that was fiercely loyal to Spain saw him as a pirate, Bouchard's legend acquired its own life, one that continued to the present day. As recently as 1964, a group of Argentine residents who proposed to pay homage to their hero inadvertently started a heated debate in Monterey. "Do We Really Want to Honor Village Pillage?" demanded a headline in the local newspaper and citizens wrote angry letters. The proposal died a quick death.

The discussion, however, brought forward new facts, and

Monument to Bouchard in Buenos Aires. Courtesy of the Departamento de Estudios Históricos Navales de la Armada Argentina, Buenos Aires.

in 1981, about two centuries after Bouchard's birth, an Argentine delegation placed a commemorative plaque on a large stone just a few yards from the site of El Castillo. Still, the local newspaper, reflecting the popular belief, announced the event as

"Monument to Pirate Hippolite Bouchard to be Dedicated." The Argentine consul general of San Francisco, the Argentine naval attaché from Washington, a number of proud Argentine exchange students, and the commander of the Presidio of Monterey attended the ceremony. To the U.S. authorities, of course, this was merely a symbolic act acknowledging something that had happened in Monterey between Spain and one of its rebellious colonies, well before Monterey became part of the United States. Nevertheless, and aware of the sensitivities of the local population, the presidio's public affairs officer took pains to explain that while the monument was dedicated to a historical event, it was not necessarily intended to honor Bouchard.

Who was this man who still provokes so much controversy?

Bouchard's dominant trait was bravery. An intensely individualistic man, he liked money as much as he disliked rules and the Spaniards. Within those constraints, he was a principled man, and his contribution to the American struggle against Spain cannot be denied. Unlike other privateers of the time, who were interested only in getting rich, Bouchard established roots in Buenos Aires, and fought bravely under San Martín, becoming a commissioned officer in the Argentine armed forces and a privateer. His job was to attack Spanish assets and promote the revolution against Spain in its colonies. He did so while following certain self-imposed rules. In his writings, when he speaks of ordering a town to be pillaged, he adds, "with the exception of churches and the American civilians' houses." The facts of his raid on California confirm that, to a large extent, he followed these rules.

Some of his actions may seem ruthless. Yet one cannot judge him by today's standards. In Bouchard's time, flogging, for example, was commonplace on land as well as at sea. There was no need for a court order; whoever was in charge of the situation could rule on it. The same holds true of the execution of mutineers and pirates in time of war—and the Buenos Aires privateers were waging war against Spain. Before executing the mutineer Griffiths in Hawaii, Bouchard called a council of his officers—essentially a court martial—and followed their advice.[25] Bouchard was more ruthless with the Malayan pirates—he had them eliminated against the recommendation of his officers.

As the distinction between a privateer and a pirate was a fine one, accusations of piracy were common. Bouchard, however, was never convicted of piracy. The Argentine naval historian Burzio perhaps characterizes Bouchard best when he calls him "the greatest of our privateers."

Solá

Solá remained a fierce royalist to the end of the Spanish rule. As late as January 1822, when the Mexican revolutionaries had already triumphed without his knowing about it, Solá wrote to a colleague in Baja California that he had received from Mexico "such documents as are printed in a country of dreamers, since independence is a dream . . . you and I, aware that the immortal, incomparable Spanish nation has many and great resources with which to make herself respected, must look with contempt on such absurd views."[26]

In March 1822, after a delay of six months, news of the victory—and with it the end of the Viceroyalty of New Spain—reached Alta California. The victor was not a popular guerrilla like Hidalgo but the conservative Agustín de Iturbide, who eight months later would become Agustín I, the emperor of Mexico. In a surprising turnaround, Solá and his subjects renounced their allegiance to Spain and embraced the new order. With his transformation complete, Solá wrote to his cousin in June 1822, announcing that he was coming to Mexico, and rejoicing in the triumph of independence.[27] He was elected to the Mexican congress and left for Mexico in November 1822. Apparently, he was not admitted to the congress, however, he did serve on a commission for the promotion of California's economy. In 1826, Solá was separated from military service by the Mexican government.[28] Since by then he was sixty-five years old he was probably retired. After that, he disappears from history.

Unlike Bouchard, Solá, the defender of Alta California, has no monuments erected to him in Monterey. However, José de Jesús Vallejo, the artilleryman of Monterey, even though the governor ignored his bravery during the Bouchard raid, paid Solá the following tribute when he wrote half a century later, "Christian piety, love for his neighbor and adherence to the laws of Spain were the qualities that distinguished the old colonel. He was the first government official who tried to promote education of the Californios and although a thoroughly Spanish nobleman, there is no doubt that he loved the Californios as if they were natives of his own homeland."[29]

Corney

In 1820, after an absence of seven years, Peter Corney arrived in London. Later, he wrote about his experiences, including his association with Bouchard, for the London Literary Magazine. In 1836 he was named to a responsible position with a trading company of British Columbia. He died on board the ship that was taking him to assume that position. The ship's name was *Columbia*—the name of the ship on which he made his Pacific coast voyages in the 1810s.[30]

Alta California

For the *gente de razón*, independence meant freedom of commerce—something they had always longed for. For the unfortunate Indians, it simply meant that their white masters had changed. Monterey and San Diego became open ports, and trade in hides, tallow, and grain with non-Spanish vessels blossomed. Foreign immigration increased, and more whitewashed adobes with red roofs sprang up at random around the Presidio of Monterey. The place was developing into an agreeable pueblo—enough so to impress Richard Henry Dana, Jr., who, when visiting the California coast fifteen years after Bouchard's raid, wrote, "Monterey, as far as my observation goes, is decidedly the pleasantest and most civilized-looking place in California."[31]

Not much that is visible remains in Monterey of the period described in this book—with the notable exception of the San Carlos Cathedral. It is a true relic of Spanish California and one of the last remnants of the place where the Royal Presidio of Monterey, the first seat of California government, once stood. Governor Solá, a deeply religious man who lived only a few yards away, often visited it. Even Bouchard, a Catholic himself, may have done so. Today, the San Carlos Cathedral is the oldest continuously functioning house of worship in California.

Appendices

1. Translation of Bouchard's manuscript

This is a translation of the manuscript in which Hipólito Bouchard's narrates his voyage around the world. The account is in the form of a trip report to his superiors in Buenos Aires. Bouchard, a Frenchman, dictated the report in Spanish to his scribe, the sixteen-year-old apprentice pilot Tomás Espora. The source document used for the translation is a photocopy of the original manuscript in the Archivo General de la Nación in Buenos Aires.[1] The source document is difficult to read because of the partially illegible penmanship, and numerous spelling errors. Fortunately, an Argentine naval historian, Pablo Arguindeguy, provided me with a transcription of the manuscript. I used this transcription, accurate with only a few exceptions, and the photocopy of the original manuscript to translate Bouchard's narrative.

In translating, I made certain changes from the original. The dates in the original are often inaccurate, but as they do not affect the essence of the story, they were left unchanged, with one exception: Bouchard dated his report February 10, 1818, but the year was 1819, and I have changed it accordingly. The original manuscript uses Spanish phonetic spelling for names of places. Wherever possible, I have translated these names to English. For Bouchard's officers, I used the names listed in the document that describes the officers and supplies of his vessel, *La Argentina*, at the time of her departure from Buenos Aires.[2] Paragraphs were left as in the original, and units of measurement were translated into their English equivalents. The few words that were illegible in the original are indicated with three ellipsis dots . . . Finally, the words in brackets are mine.

Your Excellency [3]

Fulfilling my duties as your subject I have the honor of putting this report in your hands. I have not done so earlier because I did not find any vessels heading for Buenos Aires and even less having some . . . to report about my situation. I have run from one extreme to the other but did not have the luck of finding a single ship with the Spanish flag since my departure from Buenos Aires on June 27, 1817, up to my arrival at the islands of Tres Marías on the coast of Baja California.[4]

On June 27, 1817, I departed from the buoys of Buenos Aires toward the island of Madagascar to get food and water. On the 4th of September I cast anchor in one of the ports of an island called Tamataba [Toamasina] where four vessels were involved in slave trade. At this port, an officer of his Majesty of Great Britain was trying to prevent such a trade. He requested, through my second Don Nathan Somers, that I help him should these ships attempt to embark some Negroes. This was, he said, because he did not have enough armed forces to fulfill his obligations while awaiting an [English] corvette that was on her way to this coast to prevent such actions. I offered him all the forces under my command and said that I would do all I could to prevent such a vile commerce, by virtue of the treaties with the European Nations and the high aims of Your Excellency, which are to abolish, within your reach, all forms of slavery. Although several Negroes have already been boarded on some of the ships, I took the necessary precautions to avoid further boarding until the arrival of the corvette *Comwai*, which, at her arrival, would take charge of the four vessels. On the 14th of September, having replenished my food and water supplies and intending to leave the next day, I asked the English deputy to take possession of papers that I was sending to the governor of the island of France where it was described how I prevented the boarding of the Negroes on three English and one French vessel. The next day the English corvette appeared in front of the port, which forced me to stay until the 16th. As soon as she anchored I conveyed to her the detention of the slave vessels, and on the same day at 11 in the morning I departed for the coasts [of Bay] of Bengal. On the 18th of October, I sent a boat to inspect[5] an American frigate coming from Bengal and learned that for the past three years Spanish vessels of the Compañia de Filipinas had stopped doing business in that port.[6] With this news, I decided to cross the Sunda Strait. During the voyage from the island of Madagascar to the Sunda Strait I was struck by an outbreak of scurvy. The numbers [of casualties] were quite high, as during one day 84 sick men were lying in their cots without being able to move, and this is without counting the poor wretches who died in the strait. I can assure Your Excellency that the perseverance and desire to fight the oppressor of the Americas conquered all the difficulties in my voyage. On the 7th of November, I anchored in an island called Nueba Isla at the head of the island of Java. The following day I sent all the sick men ashore to a prepared tent, hoping that some would improve. After eight days, noticing that nothing had been achieved, I ordered my surgeon to have the sick buried up to their necks in holes four feet deep. The next day I went ashore and saw them all being buried. The result was that those who were totally infected died within an hour; the rest did improve. This procedure was repeated many times until the poor men could regain the use of their limbs. On the 18th of November, I departed toward the island of Luconia [Luzon, Philippines] by crossing the Macasan [Makassar] Strait. The 7th of December, while in the middle of the strait, we noticed five approaching proas. At noon, one of them boarded our ship on the port side. While boarding, they raised a black flag, forcing us to defend ourselves with firearms, sabers and knives. We could not use our battery guns because we lacked able-bodied men: those who had recovered from scurvy had been further decimated by an attack of dysentery. Also, I failed to pay attention to this type of boat even though I had noticed many pirates in this strait. After one and one-half hours of fighting I saw the proa's captain commit suicide by stabbing himself twice and jumping in the water. Five others followed his example after realizing that they could not achieve their objective. After the loss of their chief, and terrified by the moaning of the many wounded, the rest of them fought for only a very short time.

On my side there were seven wounded, including two officers: the Second Commander Don Nathan Somers, the First Lieutenant Don Luis Crassack, the boatswain,[7] and four sailors. When the firing stopped, I ordered a few men to jump aboard the proa and have all people that might be hiding come up on the bridge deck. To my surprise, 42 men came up, without counting the men who had killed themselves or the ones we had killed. The majority were wounded and also in chains, yet they seemed not satisfied, and something was left in their hearts to try for a second time. As soon as I realized their intentions I called my officers and asked their opinion. Each answered that, as pirates, they needed to be punished but as most were wounded, to let them go. To this I decided to keep some of the young men but throw the others on the proa, cut their masts and open fire at them with the upper battery. This was immediately executed. Upon noticing this, the other four proas, which did not participate in the fight because the wind was calm, fled. I can assure Your Excellency that had I had favorable winds or had they attacked other ships, as they attack seven or eight a year, having just recently taken a Portuguese ship and killed them all [I would have punished them.][8] With this journey over, I headed for the island of Solis to get provisions and refresh the sick on board. On January 2, 1818, I anchored in the port of that island but became apprehensive when I realized that everyone seemed of the same breed as those from the proas; it was with some difficulty that I got some provisions. The 7th of the same month I sailed for the island of Luconia [Luzon], and after twenty days of navigation I encountered an English merchant frigate sailing from Bengal to Manila. I sent a boat to inspect the vessel, and not finding any papers proving that the cargo belonged to the Spaniards, I let her proceed to her destination. However, I firmly believed that upon her arrival she would inform the Government of my presence even though I took all the necessary precautions so she would not recognize me.

On the 31st of January, I started cruising in front of the port of Manila and up to the 30th of March I seized sixteen vessels that were carrying nothing but sugar and rice. I sank them all. From some prisoners I learned that the troops in Manila were reduced to eating only small rations of rice. Having learned that a ship of the Compañía San Fernando y el Rosel[9] and a war corvette were inside the port of Manila, I assumed that a few days after learning of our presence some of the ships would come out to prevent my cruising. Consequently, I took the necessary precautions, with the most demanding vigilance, so as not to be surprised at night by the three vessels.[10] I can assure Your Excellency that had one of the three [vessels] come out they would have tasted Argentine anger, even though I was left with few people after this painful voyage. We had all agreed to perish rather than fall into the hands of the Spaniards, but the miserables, instead of coming out, kept the ships inside and embargoed all commercial ships of the island of Luzon. I cruised for three months in front of them without a single ship daring to leave. On the 30th of March I decided to abandon my cruise in front of the port of Manila and continue cruising north of Luzon island in the Canal de los Galeones. On the 29th of that month we sighted a brigantine coming from the Marianas islands. They were close to shore, with calm winds, near the port of Santa Cruz [Philippines]. As soon as they saw us they turned around and had their boats tow them into the port. Seeing the impossibility of getting closer with my ship, I armed three boats, putting the first under the command of my Second

Don Nathan Somers, the second under Don Luis Crassack and the third under Don John Vamburgen. The first boat, being the best armed, left before the others and approached the brigantine. When the boat came within range of the brigantine's cannons both sides started firing, but the boat's firearms[11] could not damage the brigantine. The first boat continued the pursuit, and as soon as the brigantine anchored, they boarded her. Meeting fierce resistance, the boat had the misfortune of turning over, and the defenseless men in the water were murdered with spears. The first to be killed was my Second Commander Somers. The other two boats tried to help the men in the water; those who could swim reached the shore and five of them were rescued. One of these men, pierced through by a spear, died as soon as he came aboard. The remaining fourteen men were murdered in the water using the worst kind of cruelty one can see in this world. When the two boats returned, I was informed of it all. With my ship, I could not reach the place where it happened so that I could avenge these murders, therefore, I decided to go to a port six leagues away, where they had some small schooners. I sent an armed boat to get some of these vessels so as to have them armed and avenge the murders committed by these bandits. I named Don Luis Crassack to execute this task. At eight in the evening he departed from our ship and by 11 he had completed his assignment. At once, I had the schooner moored next to us and armed her with one short gun of 12 plus other guns of small caliber and the necessary supplies. I named Lieutenant Don Daniel Oliver and Señor Don Luis Crassack along with 35 men to seize the brigantine. The schooner departed at dawn of the same day. In the afternoon of the following day they seized the brigantine, which had been abandoned by the murderous cowards as soon as we started firing at her. The enemy officers and crew were now ashore along with 200 armed men consisting of peasants and soldiers. With a cannon of 4 they started firing at the brigantine, which Don Daniel Oliver had seized. As the firing was preventing the removal of the brigantine, the schooner got closer to shore, firing at the enemy. Everyone ashore fled, abandoning their cannon and some dead and wounded. Now the brigantine and the schooner departed without suffering any losses. With this affair finished, I continued sailing toward the north of the island. On the 13th of March I seized a schooner sailing towards the island of Batan [Philippines] with a cargo of the king. A strong wind blew from the NE, and all I could do was to send eight sailors and one of my officers on the schooner to get the prisoners back on my vessel.[12] Since it was impossible to send the boat back to the schooner, I signaled them to follow me all night, signaling that in the morning I would issue the appropriate instructions. The next day the bad weather continued and I still could not communicate any orders. Therefore, I continued sailing toward my destination accompanied by the prize for the entire day. During the night of the 15th the prize disappeared, and up to this date I have not heard of her. I firmly believe that they went to Macao or Canton because of their greed for the silver and other goods that were aboard. The strange thing is that the schooner has no papers. Four days after the disappearance of this ship I asked Lieutenant Oliver, who was commanding the brigantine, whether he knew anything about the schooner.[13] He answered that he had not seen anyone since he became separated from us because of the strong winds that he experienced from the 10th till the 18th. I issued the order that in case we got separated before reaching the port of San Iloefonso [Ildefonso, Philippines], where I was heading to get fresh food and to put the sick ashore, he should know that I would stay there for 12 to 15 days. If by any chance he was forced to part company from me, he could rest assured that he would find me anchored in that port. However, if after 15 days he did not show, I would sail away. He answered that he would do everything in his power not to get separated and that the information he had received made things clear about what he was to do in case of separation.

He did follow me until the 6th of May. On the 8th I entered the port of San Iloefonsom [Ildefonso] and stayed there until the 21st. Several times I sent a boat outside the port to look for signs of the brigantine but in vain. Even though I took the necessary precautions on land and sea, I could not get the brigantine to join us, and up to this date I have never heard of her again. I assume that the brigantine is now under the command of Your Excellency and that you would have learned of the enormous sufferings I went through up to the date the brigantine separated from us.[14] Under these circumstances I still had the captured captain of the schooner with me. I asked him what ships of the Compañía de Manila were navigating, to which he answered that for the past three years no Compañía ships of the Acapulco and San Blas route had come to Manila. He did not know why. During that time, he said, the Compañía de Filipinas had sent three commercial vessels to Peking to get the freight that for a long time had been arranged with that city. With this news, and considering that the vessels of the Compañía de Acapulco y San Blas were halted and that because of the revolution in Mexico the Compañía de Manila was not transporting silver anymore, I decided to head for the area of Peking, and on the 21st of May I departed from the port of San Ildefonso on the eastern coast of Luzon. Between the 24th and 29th of the same month I was hit by a storm and the sick men, who earlier had improved, reverted to their previous condition to the point that there were days when as many as three men died. Nevertheless, I continued up to a latitude of 40 degrees and 41' north. Noticing that the number of sick were increasing and the supplies were diminishing I decided to head for the Sandwich Islands [Hawaii], which were the last islands discovered by Captain Cok [Cook] and the place where he was murdered. On the 18th of August we sighted these islands and on the 18th at 3 in the morning some natives of the island approached us in a canoe and came aboard. One of them spoke some words in English and told me that at midnight a vessel had left the port and that another ship was in the port. This ship, which had 18 cannons, had been a Spanish ship but now she was owned by the King [Kamehameha I] of that island. I did not know what to do, an armed Spanish vessel in the hands of these barbarians. At 4 in the morning I sighted a ship leaving the port. As the wind was calm I sent one of my boats with Lieutenant Don Guillermo Sheppard to inspect her and at the same time to find out more about the Spanish ship in the port of Karakakau [Kealakekua Bay].[15] He executed the orders at once and having learned about the ship came back aboard. He informed me that the corvette anchored in the port was the *Santa Rosa de Chacabuco*[16] and that the reason she had came to these islands was that her crew had mutinied off the coast of Chile, throwing the officers ashore [in Chile] and selling the corvette to the king of this island. The crew was spread across the seven islands. I at once sent the boat to the frigate, which was American, asking her to anchor in the port that she had just left and to give me an exact account of what had happened on board the *Santa Rosa*.

The officer returned saying that he had conveyed my orders and the answer was that the frigate did not have men to maneuver a ship. Seeing that instead of returning to the port she was leaving, favored by a land breeze, I got in a boat and went on board the frigate. The moment I arrived, I begged[17] him [the captain] to shorten the sails, turn around and go back and anchor in the port he had just left. This he did in disgust, turning the ship around. I begged him to assemble his crew to see whether he had any men from the *Santa Rosa*. He called for the entire crew, but seeing that they were so few I asked whether there were no more people than the ones present. Embarrassed, he answered that he had a few more men but that they were passengers going to the island called Mohoohy.[18] I begged him to have them all come up, but when this did not happen, I ordered Don Tomas Espora and all the sailors from my boat to visit the hold[19] and to bring up all those they could find. They went down at once and pulled out nine men belonging to the corvette *Santa Rosa*. I recognized them at once and had them embarked on the boat with all their clothes. Returning to my ship, I had them put in the bar[20] and then called them one by one to take their depositions. According to everyone's testimony, the leaders of the mutiny were on a different island called . . . At 11 in the morning of the 18th of August I anchored in the port and saw the corvette in very poor condition and with all her supplies ashore in possession of the king of the island. The next day, having learned all the details about the mutiny, I embarked in a boat and went for a distance of 7 leagues to where the king lived.[21] At 2 in the afternoon I got to speak with him. Through some Americans who spoke the language, I made him understand that the corvette he possessed was a vessel that had been seized by sailors who had mutinied against their officers. Because of this I had came to claim the ship and all that belonged to her. In addition, I begged him to hand over all the sailors who belonged to the *Santa Rosa* crew. He answered that he could not give up the ship because he had bought her for 60,000 pounds[22] of sandalwood and that the men of said ship had caused him many expenses. He would hand her over only if I reimbursed all that he had spent including the cost of maintaining all these men that were in his Domains. Therefore, he could not agree to anything that I was claiming. Given this answer, I did not know what to do because of the great need I had for food and water. Finally I decided to sacrifice all I could to obtain the corvette and her papers and in this manner be able to get some provisions. Pursuing this line of thought the king issued orders that I should not be allowed to get neither water nor food until he would allow it, and these orders were executed to the letter. The next day a pact was established that he would be refunded all the expenses. With the pact fulfilled on the 26th of August I took charge of the corvette, which was in the most miserable condition that Your Excellency can imagine, as much for her sails as her ropes. As for armaments and ammunition, they were so scarce that I was forced to give her some from my own ship; the few rifles they gave me were totally ruined. I made a very precise inventory of everything I received. Fearing that I would harm him after getting the corvette and provisions, the king sent me a message saying that he had no food to give me in this island and that it was the plentiful island of Mohooy where I could get everything I needed. In addition, he said, part of the *Santa Rosa* crew was on that island. In view of this, I sailed for the island of Mohooy on the 6th of September. The king gave me one of his chiefs to give the order to sell me food supplies. On the 8th, I anchored in that island and in four days of stay I got some provisions and they handed me nineteen men of the *Santa Rosa*'s crew which cost me more than had I bought them as slaves. On the 12th of the same month I set sail for the island of Whaoo.[23] arriving on the 13th and here I finished getting my water supply. On this island we captured some more men, and on the 30th I headed for the island of Atohay[24] where I anchored on the 1st of October. This is where on the 18th of September, and based on information I got in the previous island, I had sent my officer Don Jose María Piriz aboard an American Frigate with instructions to seize the leaders of the mutiny. As a result, a chief of the town of Ohahay[25] was dispatched to tell the king of this island to imprison the men in his Domains until my arrival. A portion of them had left for Canton with a brigantine they had seized by the coast of Panama. Five of them had remained on the island, and as soon as the officer whom I had commissioned told the king that he was there to imprison the men of the brigantine or the corvette *Santa Rosa*, they were captured and put in chains on the bridge. When I arrived, the commissioned officer reported to me that the brigantine had departed on the 29th of August, but that due to a dispute among the mutineers, five had stayed behind and were now imprisoned in the fort. I went ashore at once to find out where the brigantine had gone and they all said that it was toward Canton. I returned aboard and had an indictment prepared against the sailor Henrrique Gribbin [Peter Corney calls him Griffiths]. With the indictment ready I gathered all the officers to conduct a court martial against this man. He was sentenced to death. In the morning of the next day the culprit was to be placed in isolation to await execution,[26] however, during the night the king himself let him escape. On this news I went ashore and told the king that if within six hours he did not deliver this man he should bear the consequences. He asked what consequences might they be, since for every shot of mine he would send back twenty four, as that was the number of cannons he had installed at the fort. In reply to such an answer I got in my boat and returned to my ship. I at once gave the order to ready the battery and to heat up fifty cannonballs in the forge. Having a good shore breeze, I ordered the corvette to get ready for combat with her guns trained on one corner of the fort, while I would train my guns on the other, and to wait for the time I had given to open fire. After my violent departure the king had second thoughts, and in order to find out what I was up to, he sent one of his chiefs to observe the activities on board the ships. The man went back to the king with an account of what he had observed. One hour later the king sent me a canoe with the message that the next morning at eight, for certain, he would deliver the criminal to me. That is how things were left without starting the dance [hostilities]. At four in the morning, when the wind was blowing inshore from the sea, I raised the sails and waited until the time to start the attack. While I was maneuvering in front of the fort at a distance where cannonballs could be effective, the king sent me a canoe letting me know that the criminal was at the fort, and since the previous day I had embarked all my men, it seemed that what I had told him were not empty words. As soon as he said that the culprit had been imprisoned, I went ashore with some officers from both ships, and at exactly eight o'clock they turned the criminal over to us. We read him the declarations,[27] and not being obliged to answer anything he said only that they were all accomplices in the mutiny. He was given two hours to make his peace with the Almighty and to perform the duties of his religion, and at eleven on the 6th of October he was shot. I embarked at once and headed toward the island of Whao, where two men from the *Santa Rosa* resided. They had escaped the night before I left that island and I recovered them at Mohooy. On the 25th of October I sailed from these islands toward the Alta California coast, and on the 22nd of November we anchored in the Bay of Monterey, Capital of Alta California.

During the voyage from the islands to the coast of California I ordered Don Pedro Corney, whom I had put in command of the corvette, to get the boats into good condition and when approaching the port [of Monterey] to raise the American flag. As he had visited this port several times before, he should then go ashore and observe how strong were the enemy forces on land and also any other facts that could be contrary to our intentions. At night, I would get as close as possible to protect the landing. At five in the afternoon I was two leagues from shore when the wind died and we could not maneuver. We launched the boats in the water, and the frigate was towed until eleven at night and finding myself in a depth of 15 fathoms, we anchored. I sent the boats at once to the *Santa Rosa* in order to disembark immediately with two-hundred men armed with rifles and spears and entrusting the expedition to the First

Lieutenant Don William Sheppard while I waited for a breeze to get closer to the fort. The corvette was anchored at one pistol shot [less than a quarter of a mile] from the fort. I was anchored two miles from her and unable to come closer because of the calm wind and the current pulling away. All the troops from the boats and the majority of the *Santa Rosa*'s marines gathered aboard the corvette with orders to jump ashore at once and surprise the fort. Had this order been executed, the fort would have fallen without a rifle shot. Instead, the undertaking was executed quite the opposite of my orders. As soon as the boats reached the corvette, the officers went aboard and stayed inside the cabin waiting for the light of the day. At dawn they came up on the deck and at once got ready to open fire. With all the troops and marines aboard the corvette, they hoisted the flag of the fatherland and opened fire. The enemy armed forces came to the fort at once and started firing at the corvette. After seven rounds of fire I saw with disgust our flag being lowered and people escaping in boats toward my ship, four or five per boat. On my ship [at the time] there were only 40 men including myself and the last of the ship's boys. Your Excellency can deduce how I got into such a situation. Even all this could not dampen my spirit and favored by a small breeze, I set sail at once to come closer to the fort. I got within a cannon shot but was forced to anchor to avoid being pushed away by the currents. Realizing that because I was far away I could achieve nothing with my cannons, I secured the flag of the fatherland and the flag of truce and sent an officer in a boat to go ashore, away from the reach of the fort guns, to find out if they would agree to negotiations. Six or seven mounted soldiers approached the boat's landing place and were asked whether the

Señor Governor would receive a note of negotiation. They answered that they would report it at once and bring the answer back. The answer was yes, therefore, I sent the note with Don Bernardo Copacabana and I am now sending to Your Excellency a copy of the original note and a copy of the answer.[28] In these circumstances I remained all day without making any decisions, waiting for the night to undertake the removal of the people from the corvette. During the entire day, the Spaniards did not do anything to remove any of the prisoners from the corvette. It was fortunate that those ashore did not have a single boat to come aboard the *Santa Rosa*. All they did was shout at the corvette—if you do not furl [take in] your sails and lower the masts we will start shooting and sink you. While saying this they started shooting with cannonballs and grapeshot, piercing the corvette from one side to the other. Because of the shooting, the Spaniards forced an officer and two sailors from the corvette to come ashore in a small boat. As soon as they jumped ashore, the Spaniards started striking them with their sabers, taking the mistreated men to the presidio. Meantime, aboard the *Santa Rosa*, they were furling the sails and striking [lowering] the masts. So went the day of the 23rd of November. At nine in the evening I sent two boats to the corvette to rescue all the people they could, provided this were possible and that the night would allow for such an undertaking. The officer Don Juan Whuboon was the first one to go. He took a whaling boat and returned with the boat full of people, also letting me know that the Spaniards were dancing at the fort. Assuming that with the party and the noise they would not hear our boats, I now dispatched all the boats to the corvette. It was possible, in fact, to remove all the people. Only the wounded were left behind for fear that their moans might be heard. The next day in the morning I embarked two hundred armed men in boats; one hundred thirty with rifles and the rest with spears. The embarked officers were:

> Commander Don Hipólito Bouchard
> 1. Lieutenant Don Pedro Corney
> 2. Lieutenant Don Guillermo Telary
> 3. Lieutenant Don Juan Otto
> 4. Lieutenant Don Juan Haton
> 5. Lieutenant Don J. M. Piris
> 6. Lieutenant Don Thomas Espora
> 7. Surgeon Don Bernardo Copacabana
> Apprentice pilots Don Agustin Merlo and Don Andres Gomez
> Marine's officer Don Cayetano Merlo and
> Don Miguel Berges, who was in charge of the boats.[29]

At eight in the morning I disembarked one league from the fort, and the same day at ten the flag of the fatherland was flying at the fort's mast. The fort had ten cannons of 12. A battery below the fort intended to prevent landings had two cannons of eight, and there were also two mobile fieldpieces. Now the entire town was under my command. At eleven of the same day I ordered that all the food supplies found in town belonging to the king be sent aboard at once. I summoned Lieutenant Don Miguel Berges, the man in charge of the boats, who came at once with all of them. I had twelve men embark in one boat and ordered them to take possession of the corvette, which they did right away. As soon as they reached the corvette, they hoisted the flag of the fatherland, which had been hauled down the previous day, and had the wounded transferred to the frigate Argentina to get the help they needed. On November 24th I took charge of the town and sailed away on the 29th of the same month. I destroyed the fort, the cannons, and the presidios, with the exception of the churches and the American civilians' houses. I had all the artillery spiked, with the exception of two cannons that were needed and embarked on the corvette. The same day [the 24th] I sent all my carpenters to repair the corvette; the damage was no more than ten gunshots, the majority having pierced her from one side to the other. Having finished this journey on the 29th, I sailed toward the Rancho del Refugio, which belonged to a Spaniard who, according to the information I had, was one who had tormented Mexican patriots. On the 4th of December I anchored in that port and the same afternoon I sent 30 armed men from each of the vessels to take possession of the ranch, which was done instantly since they had all fled. The next day I went ashore and ordered the men to embark all the provisions they could find. While they were engaged in this activity, a party of Spaniards surprised one officer and two of my soldiers. The next day, seeing that they were not returning, I decided to sail away. I did so on the 7th, but first I had all the cloths and the furniture in the houses burned. Trying to get my prisoners back, I headed for the Mission of Santa Barbara, assuming that that was where they had been sent by orders from their closest leader. On the 8th I anchored at that mission where I found the prisoners. Your Excellency will find about . . . from the copy of the negotiating notes that I am sending to you.[30] On the 11th I sailed toward the Mission San Juan [Capistrano] and anchored in its port on the 16th. The same day I sent the commander of that mission a request for some provisions, to be properly reimbursed, to which he answered by word of mouth, that he had enough powder and bullets to give me. The same night I decided to send people ashore. The next day at four in the morning I sent 100 men at the command of the First Lieutenant Don Pedro Corney to take possession of the town, which he did by ten in the morning. At noon he retreated, burning the entire town and sparing only the church and the houses of the American civilians. I can assure Your Excellency that nothing was stranger than that when returning to the ships, four men, three American and one English, deserted. They were the corporal of the volunteers on board named Pedro Salonia and the sailors Nicolás Echavarría, José Cesar, and José Rost. I learned this by a note, a copy of which I am sending to Your Excellency. Believing that they had been seized, I waited until the 19th sending a note meanwhile to the commander saying that if he did not return those men I would land and burn the church and the houses of the civilians. He answered by note that the four men I was missing had come forward asking for protection of the flag under which they were born. Given this answer, I decided to leave, which I did on the 20th heading toward Cerros [Cedros] Island by the California coast. On the 24th of December, I anchored off that island in order to repair the damage to both of my ships. On the 15th of January I sent the boats to inspect a vessel that had anchored on the west side of the island, eight leagues from where I was.

The Captain of that ship gave me the good news that there had been a terrible revolution in Lima [Peru] and that the results would have been more favorable to those who had risked themselves to defend freedom, had it not been for the base condition of some who denounced them. The [Spanish] Government at once took the necessary precautions and the insurgents were apprehended. One can only surmise that they suffered a terrible punishment. I cannot give Your Excellency a more exact description of the outcome because the next day, after hearing the story of the port of Callao, the English ship sailed away. Having satisfied some of my needs, I set sail on the 17th of January toward the port of San Blas, where I intended to prevent the entry of Spanish ships. On the 25th of that month I started the blockade, and on the 26th a brigantine appeared proceeding from the port of San Juan de Nicaragua with 50 days of navigation and a cargo of Ca . . . From the brigantine's prisoners I got confirmation of the revolution in Lima. According to the declarations made by the prisoners whom I have under my control, I asked how many men had been arrested. He [they] answered that he [they] did not know for sure, only that more than 200 had been apprehended and put in the palace[31] where the viceroy of Lima lives. Some of them had conspired to set the palace afire with the help of some officers who were on guard duty. The night the prisoners were going to escape, they were given some barrels of gunpowder but were discovered. According to one of my prisoners who was present at these events, all of these prisoners were executed. Many others were persecuted. I cannot give more information than that to Your Excellency. Promising to do all that I can to get [more] information about and protect these unfortunate men, I offer my services to Your Excellency. A ship of the Compañía de Calcutta has advised me that several individuals compromised [in the Peruvian uprising] are wandering about the coast of the province of Guatemala and Nicaragua. I promise to Your Excellency to do all I can to get them out of the terrible troubles that are threatening them.

On the 31st of January, I sighted an English ship of the Compañía[32] anchored off one of the islands called Tres Marías. As soon as she caught sight of us, she sailed away, and the next day at four in the morning I sent an officer aboard to inspect her. I found her with Spanish papers relating to a correspondence with the Governor of San Blas and the Commander General of Rosario. I am sending to Your Excellency a copy of a note that I found in possession of the supercargo[33] containing some lines in its invoice that are prohibited by the laws of war. I detained him for 4 days, but given the tight regulations that Your Excellency deigned to give me before my departure, I did not dare to detain him any longer. I advised the ship's supercargo and her captain to take their cargo to the coast of Chile since I knew that those provinces lacked the products that, judging by their declarations, they had. They agreed with me that it would be more advantageous for them to go to that coast. Having agreed on this, I decided to inform Your Excellency of everything that happened on my voyage up until this date, promising Your Excellency to exert all my care and vigilance for the fate of our compatriots who are being unjustly sacrificed by the Spanish tyranny.

This is as much as I can reveal to Your Excellency. The English ship, named the *Buena Esperanza*, will leave tomorrow the 8th of February of one thousand eight hundred and nineteen, and I will continue my blockade until the need for provisions forces me to leave this port.

I am sending to Your Excellency a declaration taken from

the Captain of the brigantine *San José* alias *Las Anamis*, Don José Gregorio Ramíres, about the bad behavior of the gentleman Don Guillermo de Brown on the coast of Chocó [Colombia].[34] From this declaration Your Excellency can realize the credence you gave to the men who scorn their fortunes and lives to defend the rights of free men. This is as much information I can give Your Excellency up to this date, promising to inform you about news of enemy operations I may acquire in these coasts as well as what I think about the subject. I have learned that in the Gulf of Panama there are two war vessels and many other transports ready to embark the rest of the troops that General Murillo led on these coasts. I understand that the troops will reinforce Lima or other Southern ports. Because of the information I have and the measures I will take, I shall have the pleasure of meeting them. This information comes from solid people who hope for nothing more than the happiness of the South Americans and those who serve them. This is as much I can tell Your Excellency about this matter.

May God guard Your Excellency for many years.

Frigate *Argentina* anchored off the Tres Marias islands on the 10th of February of 1819.[35]

His Excellency

(signature) Hipaulito Bouchard

His Excellency the Supreme Director of the Provincias Unidas de Sud America

2. Translation of Solá's Report

His heart had barely stopped pounding after Hipólito Bouchard's raid on Alta California when Governor Solá sent an account of the attack to his viceroy in Mexico. Since it was good news—the province was still in Spain's firm grip—the viceroy promptly had the report published, "for the satisfaction of the loyal subjects of the King our Lord, may God guard Him." The report was published on March 24, 1819, in a special edition of the *Gaceta del Gobierno de Mexico.*[1] This was the source that I used in the following translation. The only changes that I made were to spell out the abbreviations and to translate units of measurement into their English equivalents. All words in brackets are mine.

From the Señor Governor of Alta California, Don Pablo Vicente de Sola.

Excellency—I present to the superior knowledge of Your Excellency the news about what happened in the Presidio of Monterey with two frigates belonging to the rebels from Buenos Ayres.

On the 20th of November, the lookout, who is always on duty at Point Pinos, reported sighting two vessels. I immediately issued orders to all the neighbors and militiamen from six leagues around to gather at the battery site.[2] This has been my custom since I took command of this province. With the Presidio Company troops and four veteran artillerymen I gathered forty men in total. Twenty-five were from the Presidio Company, four were the artillerymen, and eleven were militiamen. After reminding them of their duties and exhorting them to fulfill their

128

obligations, I sent them to the battery under the command of the second lieutenant of artillery Don Manuel Gomez and the ensign of the Presidio Company Don José Estrada. One of the frigates anchored at eleven at night.[3] From the battery we asked where they were coming from, the identity of the vessel, and other such regulation questions, but they answered in English, which nobody could understand. We insisted that they answer our questions and that they launch a boat to bring ashore the papers or passports with which they were navigating. Finally we could understand that they were in the process of mooring the ship, and that since the night was dark they would send a boat ashore in the morning with the requested papers. But imagine my surprise, Your Excellency, when the next morning, instead of launching the boat, she started firing at the battery with cannonballs and grapeshot. This was returned in kind by our battery and after two hours of stubborn combat by both sides, the enemy hauled down their flag, begging the battery not to fire anymore as they were surrendering. Just before hauling down the flag, they launched six boats in the water. After the flag was hauled down we noticed many people embarking in the boats and heading toward the other frigate, located on the opposite coast.[4] The frigate that anchored [near the battery], called the *Santa Rosa*, carried 28 cannons of substantial caliber while the battery of the presidio had 8 cannons of eight and six caliber. The two artillerymen and their ensign fired the battery guns[5] in such a vigorous and accurate manner that they inflicted much damage to the frigate. In this they were helped by the soldiers of the Presidio Company who, during the attack, remained in their posts with remarkable calm in spite of the many cannonballs falling on it [the battery]. As soon as the *Santa Rosa*'s flag was hauled down she was ordered to send her commander ashore, but the answer was that he had escaped with most of his people to the other frigate, called Argentina which carried 38 cannons. Her commander was Hipólito Bouchard, a Frenchman with the title of general, who was at the head of both ships. I ordered that whoever was now commanding the frigate [*Santa Rosa*] should come ashore; otherwise the firing would continue. The second in command, an American, and two sailors, one from Buenos Ayres and the other from Guinea, came ashore, and as I was unable to get anything out of them other than lies and frivolous excuses, I had them put in the guardhouse. At the same time the large frigate was approaching at full speed so I gave the orders to receive her; however, she anchored at a point where our battery could not harm her. From there, Bouchard sent me a note with one of his officers carrying a flag of truce, suggesting that I surrender the entire province. To which I replied that the governor of this province looked with due contempt on everything said in that note; that the great monarch whom I was serving had entrusted to my authority the preservation of the province to remain under his domain; that as he was threatening with the use of his force, I would with mine make him know the honor and firmness with which I was ready to repel him; that as long as there remained a man alive in this province he would not succeed in his intent because all the inhabitants were loyal and loving servants of the king; and that they would spill their last drop of blood in his service.

Despite a heavy rain, the troops remained alert at their post all night. At eight in the morning it was noticed that the large frigate [*La Argentina*] was moving against the battery. At the same time, nine boats full of people, four with a small cannon each, were heading toward Punta de Potreros. I soon realized, Your Excellency, that the intent of the enemy was to disembark in Punta de Potreros and fire on the battery. I ordered Ensign Don José Estrada, along with the 25 men from his company, to observe the boats. But what could this officer do, without cannons, to prevent the landing? They disembarked by placing the boats on the beach near each other to protect the landing. Receiving frequent reports about the enemy movements, I learned that they had disembarked with 400 men and four cannons. Seeing at the same time the two enemy vessels dueling with our battery, what could I do, Your Excellency, in such a situation? I immediately ordered Ensign Estrada to fall back to the battery and ordered him, that if he had to retreat further, to spike all cannons, remove all gunpowder, and blow up the little that would remain. One cannon was placed on a cart and I ordered it to be taken away. As the enemy saw few of our troops where they landed, they marched in a column toward the battery using a path where they could not be harmed. Seeing that it would be reckless to wait for them, the officers carried out my orders to spike the cannons and dispose of the rest, and then retreated to the presidio, where I was located. From there we offered some resistance, although it was fruitless because we were so heavily outnumbered. Therefore, I retreated with the ammunition and troops to rancho Real Hacienda,[6] five leagues from the presidio. I was able to save two boxes of gunpowder, 6,000 rifle cartridges, one 2-caliber cannon, and the paper archives of the province. But first I ordered the families of the troops and the few neighboring citizens, to retreat to the Mission Soledad.

It is known from the declarations of the second commander [of the *Santa Rosa*] and his two companions that on the day of the battle with the frigate *Santa Rosa*, she suffered five dead and many wounded. The frigate was badly battered and had there been more artillerymen, useful cannons, and sufficient ammunition she would have been sunk, for it was not possible to board her for lack of people and small boats. In spite of the active fire, which lasted two hours, no men were lost on our side, which can almost be counted as a miracle.

After doing the wicked things the rebels do by custom, like relieving their rage by shooting the animals they found, because they could not shoot people, they stole whatever they found useful in the midst of the poverty in which these people live. They left on the 25th at night. But first they set the presidio on fire, reducing to ashes the row of houses facing north and three more houses facing south. The construction is all of adobe, with walls sixteen to nineteen feet high and a wooden framework on top to hold the tiles, which all collapsed as the wood burned. Likewise, they set afire and ruined the house of the artillerymen at the battery as well as the wooden platform on top of which the cannons were resting. We could only save two cannons in working conditions: one of caliber 6 and the other of caliber 2. They took two iron cannons of caliber 8 and destroyed the remaining ones. Three days after leaving, they cast anchor at the Rancho del Refugio in the jurisdiction of Santa Barbara at a distance of nine leagues from Santa Barbara. The ranch is located 460 yards from the beach, and they made the same landing as at Monterey. As they did not find anybody, because the inhabitants had retreated to the nearby Mission Santa Ines, they removed all the goods they could, set the ranch houses afire, and stole some seeds. They also killed cattle when they run out of time to remove them all. At this place we seized three of their men, one being a lieutenant of American nationality named Guillermo Tela.

From here, they set sail on the second day and anchored the next day with a flag of truce in the cove[7] of the Presidio of Santa Barbara. They agreed to an exchange of prisoners with the commander of the presidio, Captain Don José de la Guerra, even though they did not have any prisoners, other than a peasant from Monterey who got drunk the day they departed and whom they took aboard. They were boasting that this man was a prisoner. They set sail on the second day of their arrival, having first promised to Captain de la Guerra not to stop at any other point of the coast. This promise they did not fulfill; after two days they anchored again by the beach of San Pedro, which they left the next day, and then again they stopped at the anchorage of the Mission of San Juan Capistrano. Here they found nobody but the ensign Don Santiago Argüello in command of 30 soldiers from the Presidio of San Diego, whom, in anticipation, I had sent there because I feared the damage they might cause. The enemy came ashore with 400 men and with the same cannons [as at Monterey]. They sent the attached note to the mayor of the mission, which was received by Officer Argüello, who answered that he did not have anything but gunpowder and bullets to give them. Having advanced toward the mission, the rebels burned some wood and straw houses belonging to the neophytes and then returned on board. As a result of my orders to the commander of the Presidio of Santa Barbara, Captain Don José de la Guerra, the next day 25 soldiers arrived, along with 29 citizens. An enemy drummer with his box and three soldiers with their rifles, bayonets, and cartridge belts came forward to ask for forgiveness; they told Officer Argüello that they had come in those ships against their will and were submitting themselves to the mercy of the sovereign. The next day, the aforementioned Captain Guerra also arrived with 30 men. He challenged the enemy to come ashore, but instead, they weighed anchor the same night, and the next morning they were nowhere to be seen.

I must bring to the attention of Your Excellency the enormous hardships suffered by the worthy and loyal troops in such long marches with critical time constraints, crossing large rivers and determined to fight the enemy. But the places where the enemy anchored were so far away from one another that as soon as we got a group together to face them, even if our group numbered only half of theirs, they would immediately retreat to their ship and sail away. The distance between the first and second inlet or port where they anchored is eighty-four leagues, between the second and third, nine leagues, third and fourth, forty-six leagues, and the fourth to the last stop is twenty-eight leagues. Because of these distances, it was impossible for the troops that gathered at the first stop to reach [the second stop] before they did, even though I had lookouts posted all along the coast who were providing me with the necessary information.

In the presidio fire we lost some 2,000 pesos in soap, tallow, butter, corn, beans, blankets, cloth,[8] rice, and some other things of little value belonging to our soldiers. I lost all my furniture and other things that I need very much.

May God our Lord guard the important life of Your Excellency for many years, which I wish for the good of this province. Monterey December 12, 1818.—His Excellency—*Pablo Vicente de Sola.*—His Excellency Viceroy of New Spain Don Juan Ruiz de Apodaca.

Notes

Chapter I. California as a Colony

1   Present Pacific Grove.

2   The *Provincias Unidas del Río de la Plata (or Provincias Unidas de Sud América)* was the name given to the Spanish colony of *Virreinato del Río de la Plata*, when the victorious patriots proclaimed their independence from Spain. It consisted roughly of what is today Argentina, Paraguay, Uruguay, and Bolivia. The dominant province was Argentina, and the capital city was Buenos Aires. Sometimes the name Argentina was also used.

3   In contrast, the settlement of Baja California had begun in 1697, with the founding of Loreto.

4   Bancroft, *History of California*, 2: 208. States that when Pablo Vicente de Solá, the recently appointed governor of Alta California, traveled to Monterey in 1815, the voyage lasted "seventy-five or eighty days."

5   Gregory, "Shaping of California," 18.

6   Simmons, "Indian People," 48-49.

7   Phillips, "Indians and the Breakdown," 267. Describes efforts conducted in 1834 by the newly appointed civil administrator of Mission San Luis Rey to get neophytes back to work.

8   Bancroft, *History of California*, 1: 607,608. States that absolute title to the land was vested in the king. There was no individual ownership of land, only usufructuary titles. The natives were recognized as the owners, under the king, of all the territory needed for their subsistence. Spanish settlements were assigned up to four square leagues (6.75 square miles) of land. See also Johnston, *Old Monterey*, 37, and Hackel, "Land, Labor," 132.

9   Culleton, *Indians and Pioneers*, 144. Quotes Don Diego de Borica, governor of Alta California in 1794.

10 The criticism was not limited to the *pueblos*. The friars also objected to the behavior of the soldiers. See Castañeda, "Spanish Violence," 75. Writes of sexual violence against Indian women, "The despicable actions of the soldiers, Serra told Bucarelli in 1773, were severely retarding the spiritual and material conquest of California."

11 Bolton, "The Mission as a Frontier," 54.

12 Based on the *Annual Report on the Spiritual State of the Missions for the Year 1821*, by Padre José Señán. See Engelhardt, *Missions and Missionaries* 3: 173.

13 Engelhardt, *Missions and Missionaries*, 3: 80. Figures are for the year 1819.

14 Engelhardt, *Missions and Missionaries*, 3: 79. To provide an idea of the relative values at the time (currency is in pesos): "cattle, $2 to $6; sheep skin, $1.50; 24 large knives, $26; 4 arrobas of fine chocolate (arroba 25 lb.), $36." See also Bancroft, *History of California*, 2: 421 and Engelhardt, *Missions and Missionaries,* 3: 647.

15 Dana, *Two Years*, 80. Although this comment describes California in 1834, the custom had probably developed earlier.

16 La Pérouse, "The Journals," 82-84, 87.

17 Mornin, "Adelbert von Chamiso," 7-8.

18 In addition to smuggling, there was also official trading with non-Spanish vessels. Governor Solá allowed this trade to proceed even without the authorization from the viceroy. See Khlebnikov, *The Khlebnikov Archive*, 78, 90.

19 Not to be confused with today's Presidio of Monterey, built many years later about one mile away from the Royal Presidio.

20 Solá, "Noticia," 285. Names this ranch as "Real Hacienda." Ranchos del Rey were government-run ranches, guarded by presidio soldiers. They were in competition with the missions that provided the same products. See Bancroft, *History of California*, 1: 621, 682.

21 Corney, *Early Voyages*, 130. The "fifty houses" were the buildings within the presidio.

22 Culleton, *Indians and Pioneers*, 187-188. Writes that according to the Monterey parochial books there were six extramural Montereyans, one being Boronda.

23 Williams, *The Presidio*, 135. Provides this estimate of the external dimensions of the presidio. Howard, *Lost Fortress*, 41, cites an 1816 estimate by Alférez Estrada of 175 by 128 varas (481 by 352 feet). Another estimate is an interior plaza of 110 varas (302 feet) on each side given by de la Guerra in 1803; see Howard, *Lost Fortress*, 40.

24 Williams, *The Presidio*, 101.

25 Bancroft, *History of California* 2: 422. States that between 1810 and 1820 the military force remained constant at about 410.

26 Ibid., 379. The entire forces reporting to Monterey were eighty-one soldiers and officers, five artillerymen, one bleeder and three

mechanics. Twenty-eight retired soldiers also lived in the area, sometimes used as volunteers.

27 In addition, they were responsible for the Rancho del Rey, the Castillo battery, the Aduana (customs) and the Aduana battery and for the Pueblo of San José. See Williams, *The Presidio*, 174.

28 Spencer-Hancock and Pritchard, "El Castillo," 234.

29 Solá, "Noticia," 284: eight cannons of 6- and 8-caliber. Bouchard, "Manuscripto": ten cannons of 10-caliber. Piriz, " Memoria": eighteen cannons of 12- and 18-caliber. Corney, *Early Voyages*, 130: In 1815 there were two 6-caliber field pieces in the middle of the presidio, ten 12-caliber at the Castillo, and two long 9-caliber guns at the beach.

30 The approaching ships could determine the distance from shore by measuring the interval between the light flash through the fog from the shore guns and the time the explosion was heard.

31 Corney, *Early Voyages*, 118.

32 M. Vallejo, "Historical and Personal," 1: 103.

33 Nuttall, "The Gobernantes," 256.

34 Bancroft, *History of California*, 2: 470-472.

35 Ibid., 426.

36 La Pérouse, "The Journals," 70-71.

37 The following account is a summary of the childhood memories of Juan B. Alvarado as recounted by Hittell, *History of California*, 1: 635.

38 Khlebnikov, *The Khlebnikov Archive*, 78, 90.

39 Bancroft, *History of California*, 2: 215.

40 Ibid., 214.

41 Bancroft, *History of California*, 2: 211, 212.

42 Ibid., 224.

Chapter II. Privateering

1 Rodríguez and Arguindeguy, *El Corso Rioplatense*, 24.

2 Garitee, *Private Navy*, 224.

3 Rodríguez and Arguindeguy, *El Corso Rioplatense*, 103, 315, 316.

4 It is difficult (perhaps impossible) to determine with any precision the number of privateers. The cited number is from T. Caillet-Bois, *Historia Naval*, 145.

5 Ibid., 151.

6 Garitee, *Private Navy*, 225.

7 The United States brought charges against privateers based on Spanish allegations. But "Charges were not convictions. With frequent bills of sales, names changes on the vessels, silent owners,

multiple commissions, and prize goods altered to resemble regular importation, it was difficult to prove the Spanish charges." See Garitee, *Private Navy*, 227.

8   Rodríguez and Arguindeguy, *El Corso Rioplatense*, 26, 314.
9   Jones, "California," 4-21. Describes the attitude of the United States government and its people toward the rebel cause.
10 Bouchard signed his name Hipaulito.
11 For a brief history of Bouchard at the service of Napoleon, see O'Dowd, "Pirates and Patriots", 5-6.
12 Lajous, "Capitán de Navío," 9-10. Although the precise date of his arrival is unknown, Bouchard was at the service of the Provincias Unidas' navy by September 15, 1810. See Martí Garro, "Hipólito Bouchard," 62.
13 Mitre, *Páginas de Historia*, 69. Bartolomé Mitre was an Argentine statesman and its president during 1862-1868.
14 T. Caillet-Bois, *El Proceso*, 30.
15 Barros Arana, *Historia* 12: 312.
16 T. Caillet-Bois, *El Proceso*, 8.
17 R. Caillet-Bois, *Brown y Bouchard*, 20.
18 Floria and Belsunce, *Historia de los Argentinos*, 367. Data are for the year 1810.
19 Ratto, *Capitán de Navío*, 16-23.
20 Martí Garro, "Hipólito Bouchard," 58.
21 Ibid., 82.
22 Ibid., 67.
23 Ibid., 72, 74.
24 Émigrés had to change their first names into Spanish. Brown's original first name was William. Bouchard's Hypolite became Hipólito.
25 Martí Garro, "Hipólito Bouchard," 70.
26 Bouchard, "Comunicación."
27 R. Caillet-Bois, *Brown y Bouchard,* 35.
28 Ibid., 39.
29 For background about *La Argentina*, see Rodríguez and Arguindeguy, *El Corso Rioplatense,* 201-212.
30 R. Caillet-Bois, *Brown y Bouchard*, 41-43.
31 Ibid., 45, 46.
32 For a summary of these charges, see Rodríguez and Arguindeguy, *El Corso Rioplatense*, 171.
33 Manuscript dated November 21, 1816. Archivo General de la Nación, Buenos Aires, AGN: X.4.10.5.
34 R. Caillet-Bois, *Brown y Bouchard*, 56.
35 Griffin, *The United States*, 106. R. Caillet-Bois, Brown y Bouchard,

28, states that there were 200 captured ships.

36 Rodríguez and Arguindeguy, *El Corso Rioplatense*, 320.

37 Echevarría estimated the investment at 82,000 pesos. See Carranza, *Campañas Navales*, 3: 135.

38 On September 9, 1816, Bouchard was named Sargento Mayor de la Marina (equivalent to today's lieutenant commander). See Archivo General de la Nación, Buenos Aires, AGN: X.5.1.2.

39 After the departure of *La Argentina*, four more privateers departed Buenos Aires in 1817 to harass the Spaniards. See Quartaruolo, "El Crucero," 180.

40 Quartaruolo, "El Crucero," 172, 177. For the history of these uniforms as well as the request by Echevarría to allow *La Argentina* privateers to use them, see Luqui Lagleyze, "Apuntes," 65-70.

41 The names of Bouchard's officers are given as they appear on the list of men and supplies signed by Bouchard on the departure day of *La Argentina*. However, one name, Shippard, has been changed to Sheppard, and is so used in this book. See Bouchard, "Estado Gral."

42 Juan Martín de Pueyrredón, the head of state of the Provincias Unidas del Río de la Plata, signed the instructions.

43 Carranza, *Campañas Navales*, 3:66.

44 The captain of the *Tupac Amaru* was granted Provincias Unidas citizenship and stayed in Buenos Aires. The original name of the vessel was *Regent;* she was renamed *Tupac Amaru* when Buenos Aires granted her letter of marque. See Rodríguez and Arguindeguy, *El Corso Rioplatense*, 261-262.

45 Rojas, *San Martín,* 120.

46 Quartaruolo, "El Crucero," 175.

47 Ibid., 176.

48 Manifest by Vicente Anastasio de Echevarría. Museo Mitre, Buenos Aires, Armario 1, Cajón 11, Carpeta 5, Documento 1.

49 The main source material about the voyage of *La Argentina*, before she reached Hawaii, is Bouchard's "Manuscripto."

50 Ibid.

51 The manuscripts of the protests are in the Archivo General de la Nación, Buenos Aires, AGN: X.5.1.5. Quartaruolo, "El Crucero," 181-184, also describes the incident.

52 Bouchard, "Manuscripto." Piriz, "Memoria."

53 Bouchard, "Manuscripto."

54 Ibid.

55 Bealer cites two letters from Manila from that period that seem to verify some sort of blockade. According to one of the letters, however, there may have been several privateers off the coast. See

Bealer, *Los Corsarios*, 129-130.

56 Bouchard does not name the brigantine or the schooner

57 Bouchard spends considerable time describing his efforts to keep these two prizes and his obvious frustration at their disappearance.

58 Quartaruolo, "El Crucero," 198. The author cites Julián Manrique's account.

59 Did the knowledge that San Martín was on the Pacific coast influence Bouchard's decision to head east? If that had been the case, Bouchard's later report to his superiors would certainly have mentioned it. However, neither he, nor Piriz nor Echevarría mention any such influence.

60 Bouchard calls the Company variously "Compañía de Manila" and "Compañía de Filipinas."

61 For a more complete description of the *Santa Rosa*, see Rodríguez and Arguindeguy, *El Corso Rioplatense*, 248-250.

62 For the complete text of this letter, see Corney, *Early Voyages*, 224-225.

63 Ibid., 188.

64 Ibid., 217.

Chapter III. The Raid on California

1 T. Caillet-Bois, *El Proceso*, 21. Bouchard sailed from Buenos Aires on July 9, 1817 with a letter of marque for sixteen months that expired on November 9, 1818 while he was on route from Hawaii to California. (Caillet-Bois gives the year as 1819, which is an error.)

2 Corney, *Early Voyages*, 217. Writes that "after getting a supply of eggs, oil, etc. from the Russians, we made sail towards the bay of Monterey." The only Russian settlement in the area was Fort Ross, which had a port at Bodega Bay.

3 So far in the voyage Bouchard had lost many men and he had to replenish them however he could. As a result the composition of the crew had changed considerably. The combined crew, according to Corney, was now a mixture of about eighty Hawaiian islanders and the rest were "Americans, Spaniards, Portuguese, Creoles, Negroes, Manila men, Malayan, and a few Englishman."

4 The number of guns given for each ship varies depending on the source. Bouchard's data are used for *La Argentina*, Corney's for the *Santa Rosa*.

5 Bouchard wrote "American flag." As his purpose was deception, it certainly could not have meant the Provincias Unidas flag.

6   Bouchard, "Manuscripto."
7   Solá and Piriz call it the "battery," Corney and Bouchard calls it the "fort" and "fortaleza," but they all are referring to El Castillo. By contrast, they refer to the presidio as the "town" or "pueblo."
8   Solá, "Noticia", 283.
9   Bouchard, "Manuscripto." Judging by two maps of the Monterey Harbor (1852 and 1983), showing soundings in fathoms, there is nothing so shallow two miles from shore. If Bouchard was anchored in fifteen fathoms, he may have been two miles from Monterey (east or west) but less than one mile from shore.
10 Bouchard, "Manuscripto," writes that the distance was a pistol shot—less than one quarter of a mile. Corney, *Early Voyages*, 217, writes that "being well acquainted with the bay I run in and came too at midnight, under the fort." Describing a previous visit to Monterey, Corney, *Early Voyages*, 118, writes that "We came too in 11 fathoms sandy bottom, about a quarter of a mile from Captain Vancouver's Observatory and about the same distance from the fort [El Castillo]." However, J. Vallejo, "Historical Reminiscences," writes that both vessels remained outside the range of cannons all night, and the next morning one of them approached land just before the battle.
11 Bouchard, "Manuscripto," writes "All the boats with troops and the majority of the crew gathered aboard the corvette with orders to jump ashore at once and surprise the fort."
12 Quartaruolo, "El Crucero," 220.
13 Corney, *Early Voyages*, 130. From his visit to Monterey in 1815, Corney was aware of both the El Castillo battery and a second battery at the "landing place." Therefore, he might have anticipated a similar situation during his raid in 1818. However, the battery had been upgraded in 1817 and he might not have been aware of that change.
14 Ibid., 217.
15 At this point, because of conflicting accounts, things get confusing. The questions are how many batteries were firing at whom. The first-hand accounts are as follows:
How many batteries?
Bouchard, "Manuscripto", refers to a fort of ten guns, a "battery farther away," presumably the beach battery, and some mobile field-pieces. Solá, "Noticia," 283, mentions only the Castillo battery but he may have counted the Castillo battery and the beach battery as a single unit, both under the command of Alférez Manuel Gómez. Corney, *Early Voyages*, 218, mentions two batteries. Piriz, "Memoria," points to three batteries: the "first battery " of

eighteen guns, the "other battery," probably the beach battery, and "several other pieces of mobile artillery." J. Vallejo, "Historical Reminiscences," mentions the beach battery at his command and also the fort guns.

Therefore, it is reasonable to assume that there were two batteries, one at El Castillo and one at the beach, plus some mobile field-pieces.

Who fired at whom?

Bouchard, "Manuscripto," says that the *Santa Rosa* opened fire but not at whom. Solá, "Noticia," 283, reports that the *Santa Rosa* started firing at the battery, which returned the fire. Corney, *Early Voyages*, 217-218, says that he "opened fire on the fort, which was briskly returned from two batteries." On the other hand, J. Vallejo, "Historical Reminiscences," asserts that the *Santa Rosa* opened fire on the Presidio of Monterey. Although this is possible— the *Santa Rosa* was approximately 3/4 miles from the presidio— no other participant mentions such action. J. Vallejo leaves the impression that it was his battery that did most of the damage to the corvette. Furthermore, he said, he stopped firing at the corvette only after being ordered so by Alférez Gómez, who was a traitor in cahoots with Bouchard. Solá does not mention separately the beach battery, nor does he mention corporal J. Vallejo. It is likely that the *Santa Rosa* started firing at the Castillo and that the two batteries returned the fire. It is unknown whether the mobile field-pieces participated in the gunfight.

16 Where was the beach battery located? The direct participants who wrote their accounts shortly after the raid (Solá, Bouchard, Piriz, and Corney), do not mention a specific location. J. Vallejo, "Historical Reminiscences", writing more than a half century later, reports that Solá, after learning that the rebels were coming, had placed cannons at a place near the beach but without saying where. The non-participants are more specific: Osio, *History of Alta California*, 44, writing in 1851, mentions that a single gun had been installed in a place called Mentidero "the gossiping place." Alvarado, "History of California," 1: 170, writing in 1876, places the Mentidero on the seashore, about 600 yards from the presidio. The same source states that the beach battery was "south of the main battery, on the place of the present [1876] steamer wharf." Clark, *Monterey County*, 167-168, records that the Steamship Company Wharf, finished in 1870, became known at that time as Fisherman's Wharf. M. Vallejo, "Historical and Personal," 1: 139, writing in 1875, states that there was a "masked battery at the place then known as the Mentidero." He adds, "the improvised battery was

situated some six hundred varas [1680 feet] from the fort." I am using M. Vallejo's account to describe the position of the beach battery.

17 José de Jesús Vallejo was the older brother of Mariano Guadalupe Vallejo. Bancroft, *History of California*, 2: 229, citing later accounts by Californians, points to the beach battery as one "not included in Bouchard's plan—whence the disaster." However, Corney, *Early Voyages*, 130, reported on his 1815 visit to Monterey that "At the landing place, close to Captain Vancouver's Observatory, is a battery of two long 9-pounders", implying that the rebels were aware of a beach battery.

18 Bouchard, "Manuscripto," mentions seven shots, while Solá, "Noticia," 285, writes that it was a fight lasting two hours.

19 One iron cannonball, weighing 412 grams—less than one pound— and 60 millimeters in diameter, was found embedded in the Castillo platform. Its location shows a trajectory originating from the harbor anchorage. The size of the cannonball, suggests a small cannon of the type usually swivel mounted on the deck of a ship and used for signaling or firing a salute. The cannonball probably came from the *Santa Rosa*. See Pritchard, *Preliminary Archeological Investigations*. But the only recorded cannons on the *Santa Rosa* were 12 and 18 pounders. It is possible that small caliber cannons, used for signaling and saluting were on board of ships, but were not mentioned as part of their inventory. *Santa Rosa*, in her effort to hit El Castillo, might have tried her luck with all her cannons, including the small one.

20 Bancroft, *History of California*, 2: 229-232.

21 Solá, "Noticia," 284.

22 Piriz, "Memoria," reports "two dead and some wounded." Solá, "Noticia," 285, writes, "five dead and a major number of wounded," based on the interrogation of Joseph Chapman. Corney, *Early Voyages*, 218, mentions three dead.

23 Monterey was not the only place in Alta California lacking boats. The same situation existed at San Francisco. Mornin, "Adelbert von Chamiso," 6, cites Chamiso on his 1816 visit to San Francisco: "We drop anchor in front of the presidio, and no boat pushes out from shore to greet us, for the simple reason that on this splendid bay Spain does not possess one single boat."

24 Data provided by the National Ocean Service of the NOAA: calculation of the tides for November 20-21, 1818. The lowest tide for November 20 was at 10:13 P.M. and the highest for November 21 was at 5:40 A.M.

25 Solá, "Noticia," 284.

26 Only Piriz mentions the request for money.

27 When months later Bouchard arrived at Valparaíso, Chile, Sheppard
    was carried in chains. See T. Caillet-Bois, *El Proceso*, 12.

28 Solá, "Noticia," 285. Only Solá mentions the small cannons.

29 My conclusion is that the landing place was at Lovers Point. This
    is based on the following. Solá, "Noticia," 284, writes that Bouchard
    landed at Punta de Potreros. Bouchard, "Manuscripto", says that
    he disembarked "one league from the Fort." Corney, *Early Voy-
    ages*, 218, points to Point Pinos as the landing place. However,
    Point Pinos is an unlikely landing place because the surf condi-
    tions at the rocky Point Pinos are not good for boat landing, they
    are much better just east of it. Solá, more familiar than Corney
    with names at Monterey, had mentioned Point Pinos in his report
    as the place where the lookout saw the two ships approaching
    Monterey. As for the landing, he excluded Punta de Pinos by spe-
    cifically pointing, in the same report, to Punta de Potreros. I have
    not been able to determine where this place was. J. Vallejo, "His-
    torical Reminiscences," asserts that Bouchard landed at La Playa
    de los Insurgentes (Insurgent's Beach). His brother, M. Vallejo,
    "Historical and Personal," 1:143, says that it took place at Playa
    de los Insurgentes, which at the time of the raid was known as the
    "beach of Doña Brigida in honor of Doña Brigida Armenta." The
    Armentas had there a fruit orchard and cultivated fresh produce
    for Monterey. Clark, *Monterey County*, 286, writes that, over time,
    the present Lovers Point Beach had different names, one of them
    being "La Playa de Brigida (named from Brigida Alvirez), widow of
    Armenta." A Mexican-period map of Punta de Pinos shows a "Casa
    de Armenta" opposite and slightly east of today's Lovers Point (Land
    Case No. 169 SD, map 1185 A, at the Bancroft Library). Burgess,
    "Pirate or Patriot," 45, writes, without elaboration, that Lovers Point
    fits best the description of the landing site.
    In my opinion, the best source here is Solá: Punta de Potreros.
    The only Puntas (Points) exist west of El Castillo. Since one can
    eliminate Punta de Pinos, the most likely choice is Lovers Point,
    because of the "Armenta" link and also because it fits the "one
    league from the Fort" statement by Bouchard.

30 Only Solá mentions a landing of 400 men and a duel of the two
    vessels with the land batteries. Given that Bouchard had only
    360 men (including noncombatants) even before the casualties of
    the *Santa Rosa*, the number 400 is excessive. The number 200,
    cited by Bouchard, seems more realistic. Likewise, the dueling
    with the two vessels is improbable—the *Santa Rosa* was disabled
    and *La Argentina* was probably closer to Bouchard's disembarka-

tion point, which would place her too far to reach El Castillo with her guns.

31 The path along Lighthouse Avenue and Hawthorne Street is relatively level. To the west of Hawthorne the hills are steeper and rockier, thus harder to advance especially with four cannons. A 1852 map of the Monterey Harbor, (Monterey Harbor, NOAA) shows a path roughly along these streets.

32 Most likely the attackers reached the hill where the present Sloat Monument stands and descended at El Castillo from behind.

33 Corney, *Early Voyages*, 218.

34 Ibid., 218. These "fieldpieces" must be the "other pieces of mobile artillery" that Piriz refers to in his manuscript. It is unknown whether the defenders used these pieces the day before in their duel with the *Santa Rosa*. Corney mentions that "we took several Creole prisoners." No other source mentions these Creoles, nor do they figure in the later negotiations concerning prisoners. It is more likely that Bouchard's army "liberated the town's prisoners," as Piriz writes.

35 Solá, "Noticia," 285.

36 Piriz, "Memoria."

37 Valdéz, "Dorotea Valdéz Reminiscences."

38 Solá, "Noticia," 286.

39 Bancroft, *History of California*, 2: 234, summarizes the damage, using several sources. "The damage to the goods taken from the warehouse or spoiled was estimated at about $5000, most of which was made up pro rata next year by the missions, which trusted to providence and the royal treasury for reimbursement . . . The houses of the governor and commandant were among those partially destroyed, and the officers lost about $5000 worth of private property." Bancroft states that by April 1819, or earlier, the repairs were completed.

40 Bouchard, "Manuscripto." It is difficult to imagine how Bouchard's men could have distinguished between Spanish and American property. It is possible that that by "Americans" he means the Indians. There is no evidence, however, that the damage to the presidio was based on such distinction.

41 Valdéz, "Dorotea Valdéz Reminiscences." However, a visitor to Monterey during August of 1820, writes that the damaged structures were still being rebuilt at the time of his visit. See Khlebnikov, *The Khlebnikov Archives*, 80.

42 Bouchard, Corney and Solá recorded different dates. Bancroft concluded that it was either the 26 or 27.

43 Fernández, "Cosas de California," says that when Bouchard de-

parted, two sailors were left behind inadvertently. "These two poor souls were made prisoners by the Californios with . . . women and children demanding that they be burned alive; but the governor, a caring man, saved their lives." This statement is unsubstantiated, unless Fernández is referring to the three men from the *Santa Rosa* who were made prisoners on the second day of the raid.

44 Bancroft, *History of California,* 2: 225, 242-245. The settlers thought, probably correctly, that the rebels would harm only the Spaniards—the military officers and the friars.

45 Bancroft, *History of California,* 2: 244, 245.

46 Ibid., 243.

47 Bouchard and Corney give this date. Bancroft shows a date of December 2.

48 Bancroft, *History of California,* 2: 249.

49 Corney, *Early Voyages,* 219.

50 Solá, "Noticia," 286.

51 Bancroft, *History of California,* 2: 236.

52 Corney and Bouchard give this date. Bancroft gives December 6.

53 Corney, *Early Voyages,* 220.

54 Solá, "Noticia," 285.

55 Guerra Ord, "Ocurrencias," 5.

56 Bancroft, *History of California,* 2: 239.

57 Ibid., 235.

58 Although Bouchard does not mention it, Solá writes that, before arriving at San Juan Capistrano, the insurgents anchored overnight at the beach at San Pedro without incident.

59 Solá, "Noticia," 286, writes that 400 rebels disembarked, and that they found only the 30 soldiers from the presidio of San Diego that he had sent there.

60 Corney, *Early Voyages,* 220-221.

61 Bouchard counted four deserters and Solá three. Corney says only that they lost six men.

62 Bouchard, "Manuscripto." Piriz, "Memoria," writes that the rebels took also some prisoners, but this has not been verified.

63 Bancroft, *History of California,* 2: 286. The numbers are: thirty soldiers from San Diego; twenty-five soldiers and twenty-nine volunteers from, presumably, Santa Barbara; and thirty more from Santa Barbara who came with José de la Guerra.

64 Ibid., 237.

65 When Solá made his first report to the viceroy, he may not have known all the facts about the raid on Rancho del Refugio. However, in his second report, which is an extension to his first, he

does not mention a battle either.

66 J. Vallejo, however, received no recognition. Osio, *History of Alta California*, 44, thinks that this was because Vallejo was a Creole, and that the Creoles were not being recognized by the Spaniards.

67 Bancroft, *History of California*, 2: 264.

68 Ibid., 479.

69 Ibid., 412.

70 In the instructions to the owner of *La Argentina* by the government of Provincias Unidas (see Quartaruolo, "El Crucero," 242), one of the stated objectives was to find out whether the people supported the insurrection against Spain.

Chapter IV. Return and Exile

1 Corney, *Early Voyages*, 221.

2 Piriz, "Memoria."

3 The arrival dates for the different vessels vary. I use the dates given by Rodríguez and Arguindeguy, *El Corso Rioplatense*, 208.

4 Corney, *Early Voyages*, 223. Writes that *La Argentina* arrived in great distress for provisions and water; she had buried about forty men.

5 Barros Arana, *Historia*, 12: 311-315.

6 Thomas Cochrane, 10th Earl of Dundonald, one of the greatest of British seamen. After falling into disgrace because of illegal financial manipulations, he left Great Britain and in 1817 accepted Chile's invitation to command its fleet in its war of independence. Later he did similar service for Brazil and Greece. Returning to Great Britain, he was eventually reinstated in the navy. He is buried at the Westminster Abbey. For a description of his services in the Spanish-American wars of independence, see Dundonald, Thomas Cochrane, *Narrative of Services*.

7 Corney, *Early Voyages*, 223.

8 T. Caillet-Bois, *El Proceso*, 23, 26.

9 In his "Memoria", written on October 1, 1819, during Bouchard's trial, Piriz states that they learned of the mutiny from "several English vessels" before arriving at Hawaii, but he does not name the vessels or the place. It is likely that Piriz made this statement to help Bouchard in his trial. T. Caillet-Bois, *El Proceso*, 23, also doubts that Bouchard knew of the *Santa Rosa* mutiny at the time he was in the Sunda Strait.

10 T. Caillet-Bois, *El Proceso*, 24.

11 Barros Arana, *Historia*, 12: 315.

12 Quartaruolo, "El Crucero," 238.
13 Mitre, *Páginas de Historia*, 105.
14 Unless otherwise noted, this section is based on Burzio, "Capitán de Navío". Burzio, a member of the Argentine embassy in Perú, put together this material using, among other sources, the archives of the Museo Naval de Perú. He stresses, however, that important source material had been lost.
15 Rodríguez and Arguindeguy, *El Corso Rioplatense*, 160, 254, 255. Carranza, *Campañas Navales*, 3:135.
16 Archivo General de la Nación, Buenos Aires, AGN: X.30.2.6. Expte 872.
17 Carranza, *Campañas Navales*, 3: 135.
18 Burzio, "Capitán de Navío," 293. Cites the opinion of Germán Stiglich, a Peruvian navy man.
19 Archivo General de la Nación, Buenos Aires, AGN: X.16.5.3, (Secretaría de Rosas).
20 Bouchard's accomplishments at the service of Argentina were more highly regarded than his accomplishments at the service of Perú. Cochrane, for example, who participated in the early struggle for the independence of Perú, does not mention Bouchard in his memoirs.
21 The ranches were the San Javier and the San José de la Nazca.
22 Burzio, "Capitán de Navío," 296.
23 Ibid., 295-300.
24 Ibid., 298.
25 Treatment of mutineers was different in time of peace and time of war. In peacetime, mutineers were, ideally, taken to their home base and tried by an Admiralty Court. In times of war the punishment was immediate.
26 Bancroft, *History of California*, 2: 450.
27 Ibid., 455.
28 Ibid., 471.
29 J. Vallejo, "Historical Reminiscences."
30 Based on W. D. Alexander's preface to Corney, *Early Voyages*.
31 Dana, *Two Years*, 78.

Translation of Bouchard's Manuscript

1 Bouchard, "Manuscripto."
2 Bouchard, "Estado Gral."
3 Juan Martín de Pueyrredón, Supreme Director of the Provincias Unidas de Sud America.
4 The Tres Marías islands are off the coast of Nayarit, Mexico.

5   *A visitarla* (to visit her). This was, however, more than a visit. Privateering ships stopped vessels to inspect their papers and to determine on whose behalf, or for whose benefit, they were navigating.

6   Presumably a port in the Bay of Bengal.

7   *Contrameastre* (an experienced seaman who directs the chores aboard a vessel).

8   This is an incomplete sentence in the manuscript.

9   It is not clear whether el Rosel is part of the company name or the name of a vessel.

10 Presumably Bouchard is referring to the ship of the Compañía San Fernando y el Rosel and the war corvette he mentions above.

11 *Pedreros y trabucos.*

12 Bouchard carried three *cabos de presas*—officers who would take seized ships home.

13 Bouchard does not name the captured schooner or the brigantine.

14 Standard procedure for privateers was to send prizes back home. Obviously, Bouchard hoped that Oliver had taken the brigantine back to Buenos Aires.

15 Bouchard refers to Kealakekua Bay, on the western shore of the island of Hawaii.

16 A licensed Argentine privateer that had sailed from Buenos Aires a few months ahead of Bouchard.

17 *Le supliqué* (I begged). Given the context of the incident, " I ordered" might be more appropriate.

18 Called variously Mohoohy or Mohooy (presumably the island of Maui).

19 *Bodega* (cellar, hold).

20 *Barra* (a long iron rod used to secure prisoners).

21 Possibly Kailua.

22 Original: 600 *quintales* (one *quintal* equals 100 pounds).

23 Called variously Whaoo or Whao (presumably the island of Oahu).

24 Possibly Kauai.

25 *Vila de* Ohahay.

26 *En Capilla* (place where condemned men were placed before execution).

27 Presumably the statement of the charges and the resulting sentence.

28 Bouchard asked for the surrender of the province. The governor answered that they would defend it to their last drop of blood.

29 Three officers—Telary, Otto, and Haton—were not part of the crew that departed with Bouchard from Buenos Aires. It is likely that

these men joined Bouchard's contingent in Hawaii.

30 Bouchard exchanged the one prisoner he took in Monterey for his three men taken at the Rancho del Refugio.

31 *Fortaleza o palacio* (fort or palace).

32 The name of the Compañía is not given.

33 Person on merchant ships in charge of the cargo.

34 Presumably, Guillermo de Brown is Guillermo Brown, an Argentine naval hero. Bouchard and Brown had disliked each other since their joint privateering voyage, in 1815, off the South American coast.

35 The original shows, erroneously, the year 1818.

Translation of Solá's Report

1 Solá, "Noticia."

2 Also called El Castillo de Monterey.

3 This ship, the *Santa Rosa*, was a corvette.

4 *Contracosta* (the coast opposite the one found when approaching a peninsula). It is not clear what this means in the context of Monterey.

5 Presumably, Solá means the second lieutenant of artillery Manuel Gómez.

6 Also called the Rancho del Rey.

7 *Rada* (small bay with some protection from wind).

8 *Jerga* (thick coarse cloth)

Glossary

Brigantine   A two-masted sailing vessel, square-rigged on the foremast.

Caliber   The weight of a cannonball in pounds.

Californio   A non-Indian of Alta California.

Corvette   A sailing warship with a flush deck and usually one tier of guns.

Creole   A person of European ancestry born in America.

Cuera   A jacket of multiple layers of buckskin or cowhide used by presidio soldiers as protective armor.

Fathom   Unit of length equal to six feet.

Frigate   A fast sailing vessel heavily armed on one or two decks.

Gente de razón   Non-Indians. Literally, "people with the ability to reason."

Grapeshot   A bag of small iron balls fired from a cannon and intended to inflict wide casualties on the enemy.

League   Unit of distance. In Spanish America approximately 2.6 miles.

Letter of marque   License granted by a state to a private citizen to capture ships of another nations.

Mestizo   A person of Indian and European heritage.

Neophyte   An Indian converted to Christianity.

Pedrero   Short cannon firing rocks.

Peso   The currency in Spanish America. Equivalent to approximately one U.S. dollar in the first half of the nineteenth century.

Proa   A fast Malayan sailing boat with a flat lee side and balanced by a single outrigger.

Pueblo   A civilian village, town.

Rancho del Rey A ranch operated by the local presidio to provide provisions for their soldiers and families.

Soldado de cuera A presidio soldier wearing a protective cuera jacket.

Trabuco   Short shotgun.

Vaquero   A cowboy, usually an Indian.

Vara   Spanish unit of length equal to 33 inches.

Notes on Sources

Unlike the great events in history, for which mountains of primary sources often exist, the voyage of *La Argentina* and the raid on Monterey left little primary source material. The participants were men of limited education who did not write much.

For the reconstruction of Bouchard's raid on Alta California, two categories of primary documents exist. The first is composed of documents written by participants shortly after the raid. These participants include Hipólito Bouchard, Pablo Vicente de Solá, Peter Corney, and José María Piriz. To a large degree they all tell the same story. I have used them almost exclusively for the reconstruction of the raid. The second category consists of documents written more than a half a century after the raid, in 1875 and 1876. These accounts, told by José de Jesús Vallejo, Mariano Guadalupe Vallejo and Juan Bautista Alvarado, differ significantly from those in the first category, and they tend to exaggerate. I used these sources in only a few instances. The narrative by Antonio María Osio, written thirty-four years after the raid, is more accurate, but it contains some errors. The main secondary source used was Bancroft's History of California. Bancroft's narrative of the raid on Monterey is based on Solá's report to his viceroy. Although Bancroft was not aware of documents written by Bouchard, Corney and Piriz, he supplemented the story with valuable local historical data.

Bouchard's story is based on several secondary source documents by Argentine naval historians (Pablo E. Arguindeguy,

Humberto F. Burzio, Ricardo R. Caillet-Bois, Teodoro Caillet-Bois, Anjel J. Carranza, Francisco Lajous, Julio M. Luqui-Lagleyze, Pedro Martí Garro, V. Mario Quartaruolo, Héctor R. Ratto, and Horacio Rodríguez). Some of these historians specialized in different aspects of Bouchard's career, others in the history of Buenos Aires privateering. They all reference and quote valuable source documents in the Argentine Archives. Chilean historian Barros Arana's account of Bouchard's arrival in Valparaíso provided an independent insight into that particular event. Any short quotes that I used from these authors throughout the book I translated from the original Spanish.

For the story of Bouchard's voyage around the world, Bouchard's manuscript is the principal source, supplemented by the narratives of Peter Corney and José María Piriz.

References

Alvarado, Juan Bautista. "History of California." 5 vols.
Translated by Earl R. Hewitt. 1876. UC Berkeley: The
Bancroft Library MS. C-D 1-5 .

Bancroft, Hubert Howe. *History of California.* 7 vols. San
Francisco: History Company Publishers, 1886-90.

Barros Arana, Diego. *Historia jeneral de Chile.* Vol. 12.
Santiago de Chile: Rafael Jover, Editor, 1892.

Bealer, Lewis Winkler. *Los Corsarios de Buenos Aires, sus
Actividades en las Guerras Hispano-Americanas de la
Independencia (1815-1821).* Buenos Aires: Facultad de
Filosofia y Letras. Publicaciones del Instituto de
Investigaciones Históricas. Número LXXII, 1937.

Bolton, Herbert Eugene. "The Mission as a Frontier Institu-
tion in the Spanish American Colonies." *New Spain's
Far Northern Frontier,* edited by David J. Weber.
Alburquerque: University of New Mexico Press, 1979.

Bouchard, Hipólito. "Manuscripto de Bouchard." 1819.
Archivo General de la Nación, Buenos Aires, AGN:
X.23.2.6.

Bouchard, Hipólito. "Comunicación de D. Hipólito Bouchard
al Supremo Director, 26 de Septiembre 1816." Archivo
General de la Nación, Buenos Aires, AGN: IX.35.1.6.
Expte. 33.

Bouchard, Hipólito. " Estado Gral. del que sale de este puerto
para la mar hoy día de la fecha la Fragata Corsario *La
Argentina* al mando de su Capitán el Sargento Mayor
Don Hipólito Bouchard." 26 de Junio 1817. Archivo
General de la Nación, Buenos Aires, AGN: X.5.1.5.

Burgess, Sherwood. "Pirate or Patriot? Hypolite Bouchard
and the Invasion of California." *American West* 11.6
(1974).

Burzio, Humberto F. "Capitán de Navío Hipólito Bouchard al
Servicio de la Marina de Guerra del Peru." *Hipólito
Bouchard.* Buenos Aires: Comando de Operaciones
Navales. Departamento de Estudios Históricos Navales.

Biografías Navales Argentinas, Serie C, No 10, 1967.

Caillet-Bois, Ricardo R. *Brown y Bouchard en el Pacífico*, 1815-1816. Buenos Aires: Facultad de Filosofía y Letras. Instituto de Investigaciones Históricas, Número LII, 1930.

Caillet-Bois, Teodoro. *El Proceso de Bouchard.* Buenos Aires: Facultad de Filosofía y Letras. Instituto de Investigaciones Históricas, Número LXIX, 1936.

Caillet-Bois, Teodoro. *Historia Naval Argentina.* Buenos Aires: Emeceé, 1944.

Carranza, Anjel J. *Campañas Navales de la Republica Argentina.* 4 vols. Buenos Aires: Departamento de Estudios Históricos Navales, 1962.

Castañeda, Antonia I. "Spanish Violence against Amerindian women." *Major Problems in California History.* Boston: Houghton Mifflin, 1997.

Clark, Donald Thomas. *Monterey County Place Names: A Geographical Dictionary.* Carmel Valley, California: Kestrel Press, 1991.

Corney, Peter. *Early Voyages in the Northern Pacific.* Fairfield, Washington: Ye Galleon Press, 1965. (First published in the *London Literary Gazette* of 1821).

Culleton, James. *Indians and Pioneers of Old Monterey.* Fresno: Academy of California Church History, 1950.

Dana, Richard Henry, Jr. *Two Years Before the Mast.* New York: Signet, 1964.

Dundonald, Thomas Cochrane, Earl of. *Narrative of Services in the Liberation of Chili, Perú, and Brazil from Spanish and Portuguese Domination.* London: James Ridgway, 1859.

Engelhardt, Zephyrin. *The Missions and Missionaries of California.* 4 vols. San Francisco: James H. Barry, 1913.

Fernández, José. "Cosas de California." 1874. UC Berkeley: Bancroft Library MS. C-D 10.

Floria, Carlos Alberto, and César García Belsunce. *Historia de los Argentinos.* Buenos Aires: Ediciones Larousse, 1992.

Garitee, Jerome R. *The Republic's Private Navy.* Middletown, Connecticut: Mystic Seaport, 1977.

Gregory, James N. "The Shaping of California History." *Major Problems in California History.* Boston: Houghton Mifflin, 1997.

Griffin, Charles Carroll. *The United States and the Disruption of the Spanish Empire (1810-1822).* New York: Columbia University Press, 1937.

Guerra Ord, María de las Angustias de la. "Ocurrencias en California." 1878. UC Berkeley: Bancroft Library MS. CD-134.

Hackel, Steven W. "Land, Labor, and Production." *California Historical Society Quarterly* 76.2-3 (1997).

Hittell, Theodore Henry. *History of California.* 4 vols. San Francisco: Pacific Press, 1885-1897.

Howard, Donald M. *California's Lost Fortress: the Royal Presidio of Monterey.* Carmel, California: Antiquities Research Publications, 1976.

Johnston, Robert B. *Old Monterey County: A Pictorial History.* Monterey, California: Monterey Savings and Loan Association, 1970.

Jones, Frances Carey. "California in the Spanish American Wars of Independence: The Bouchard Invasion." M.A. thesis, University of California, Berkeley, 1921.

Khlebnikov, K.T. *The Khlebnikov Archive.* Translated by John Bisk, edited by Leonid Shur. The Rasmuson Library Historical Series, volume 5. Fairbanks, Alaska: University of Alaska Press, 1990.

Lajous, Francisco. "Capitán de Navío Hipólito Bouchard." *Hipólito Bouchard.* Buenos Aires: Comando de Operaciones Navales. Departamento de Estudios Históricos Navales. Biografías Navales Argentinas, Serie C, No 10, 1967.

La Pérouse, Jean Francois de. "The Journals of Jean Francois de La Pérouse." *Life in a California Mission,* edited by Malcolm Margolin. Berkeley California: Heyday Books, 1989.

Luqui-Lagleyze, Julio Mario. "Apuntes de Uniformología Marítima." Buenos Aires: *Revista "Del Mar,"* XXXIV, No. 129, 1989.

Manrique, Julián. "Narración del Capitán Julián Manrique." *La Tribuna,* July 19 and 20, 1869.

Martí Garro, Pedro F. "Hipólito Bouchard Granadero." *Hipólito Bouchard.* Buenos Aires: Comando de Operaciones Navales. Departamento de Estudios Históricos Navales. Biografías Navales Argentinas, Serie C, No 10, 1967.

Mitre, Bartolomé. *Páginas de Historia*. Buenos Aires: Biblioteca de *La Nación*, 1909.

Mornin, Edward. "Adelbert von Chamiso: A German Poet-Naturalist and His Visit to California." *California Historical Society Quarterly* 78.1 (1999).

Nuttall, Donald A. "The Gobernantes of Spanish Upper California: A Profile." *California Historical Society Quarterly* 51.3 (1972).

O'Dowd, Patrick. "Pirates and Patriots." *Santa Barbara Trust for Historical Preservation Quartely*, Winter (1997-1998).

Osio, Antonio María. *The History of Alta California: a Memoir of Mexican California*. Translated, and edited by Rose Marie Beebe and Robert M. Senkewicz. Madison, Wisconsin: University of Wisconsin Press, 1996.

Phillips, George Harwood. "The Indians and the Breakdown of the Spanish Mission System in California." *New Spain's Far Northern Frontier*, edited by David J. Weber. Alburquerque: University of New Mexico Press, 1979.

Piriz, José María. "Memoria exacta y puntual de todos los sucesos y méritos mas distinguidos que superamos y labramos el señor Comandante de la fragata de guerra Consecuencia Don Hipolito Bouchard y yo . . . ," known as the "Manuscripto de Piriz." 1819. Museo Mitre, Buenos Aires, Armario 1, Cajón 11, Carpeta 6, Documento 1.

Pritchard, William E. *Preliminary Archeological Investigations at El Castillo, Presidio of Monterey, Monterey, California*. C.C.A.F, 1968.

Quartaruolo, V. Mario. "El Crucero de *La Argentina* 1917-1819." *Hipólito Bouchard*. Buenos Aires: Comando de Operaciones Navales. Departamento de Estudios Históricos Navales. Biografías Navales Argentinas, Serie C, No 10, 1967.

Ratto, Héctor R. *Capitán de Navío Hipólito Bouchard*. Buenos Aires: Secretaría de Estado de Marina. Departamento de Estudios Históricos Navales. Biografías Navales Argentinas, Serie C, No. 2, 1961.

Rodríguez, Horacio, and Pablo E. Arguindeguy. *El Corso Rioplatense*. Buenos Aires: Instituto Browniano, 1996.

Rojas, Ricardo. *San Martín, Knight of the Andes*. Translated by Herschel Brickell and Carlos Videla. New York: Cooper

Square Publishers, 1967.

Simmons, William S. "Indian People of California." *California Historical Society Quarterly* 76.2-3 (1997).

Solá, Pablo Vicente de. "Noticia de lo acaecido en este presidio de Monterey con dos fragatas perteneciente a los rebeldes de Buenos Ayres." *Gaceta Extraordinaria del gobierno de Mexico*, Tom X. Núm. 37 (24 de Marzo de 1819).

Spencer-Hancock, Diane, and William E. Pritchard. "El Castillo de Monterey: Frontline of Defense." *California Historical Society Quarterly* 68.3 (1984).

Valdéz, Dorotea. "Dorotea Valdéz Reminiscences." 1874. UC Berkeley: Bancroft Library MS. C-E 65:8.

Vallejo, José de Jesús. "Historical Reminiscences of California." 1875. Translated by Brother Henry De Groote. Edited by Elinor Butler Kern. UC Berkeley: Bancroft Library MS. C-D 16.

Vallejo, Mariano Guadalupe. "Historical and Personal Memoirs Relating to Alta California." 5 vols. 1875. Translated by Earl R. Hewitt. UC Berkeley: Bancroft Library MS. C-D 17-21.

Williams, Jack S. *The Presidio San Carlos de Monterey: The evolution of the Fortress - Capital of Alta California.* Tubac: Center for Spanish Colonial Archeology, Technical Publication Series, Number 1, 1993.

Archives

Archivo General de la Nación, Buenos Aires, Argentina.

Bancroft Library, University of California, Berkeley, California.

Departamento de Estudios Históricos Navales, Division Biblioteca y Archivo, Buenos Aires, Argentina.

Museo Mitre, Buenos Aires, Argentina.

Index

A

B

C

D

E

Peter Uhrowczik was born in Czechoslovakia, spent his teen-age years in Argentina, and has lived in California since 1963. He reconstructed the story of the raid on California and the fall of Monterey using accounts written by the participants of these events. Peter has three daughters and lives with his wife Tedi in Los Gatos, California.